TRIANGLE KIDS
Lost In A Closed System

by

Dan D. Anderson

ISBN: 978-1-257-09376-2

Introduction

The following story is dedicated to a population of children coping with the struggles of a hostile parent in custody-related matters. At a time when survival and security defenses are on high alert, children are encouraged to use their words to express where 'it hurts.' But the realities of a closed system teach children (and families, teachers, health care providers, politicians ...) to say nothing. The result: a microcosm of kids suffering from learned helplessness.

To all parents and children that continue to cope: I hope you find validation in this advocacy project. Surmount stigma, promulgate your story and hardship will lessen.

Have you ever had professional counseling? If so, perhaps you've asked yourself questions like, "What can I expect from this?" and "Will my disclosures seriously be kept confidential?"

Expectations might be unclear, giving therapy a mysterious feel from the start. As a teenager, I wondered if shrinks could read minds. But it didn't take long before I realized it had nothing to do with tricks or super powers. I found it to be a little about surveying options and a lot about accountability.

Therapists don't share one particular practice style, as you may already know. Some can have a very serious style; pretending to be naïve or agreeable is most patronizing. I believe people can tell when a therapist is genuine. But then, sometimes, it's all too obvious when they don't care at all. We can't pick on yawning too much because it's natural. But most people cover their mouth or do chin quivers if they're making any decent attempt at covering it up.

Like it would be for most teens, it made me very skeptical.

"Your Mom left me a voice ...(yawn)... a voice...mail saying that your interims had three Ds on it. Does that sound accurate to you?"

"Actually, one of those is a C. The teachers are planning to talk to her tomorrow, I'm pretty sure."

"You were suspended last week for something.... What was that about again?"

I didn't like feeling interrogated, either. My defenses were built from recent life experiences. So, like a pitcher stepping off the rubber, I sat back to settle myself before delivering to an intimidating batter. I gave a tight squint, the one I gave my catcher three years earlier in Little League. Here's the wind up, and the pitch:

"Suspended? Who said that?" I demanded.

One of my friends revealed that counselors don't do too well with confrontation. He coached me to take on a "customer's always right" stance. He'd say "you're their 'bread and butter', man." The problem is that this same friend giving advice didn't have my mom for a mom.

Mine approached me at the drinking fountain after meeting with my therapist one evening.

"What kind of thing was that you said in there today?" she asked.

Staring into the stainless steel backdrop of the drinking fountain, I could feel my heart downshifting. A smooth pitter-patter hurled into what felt like a hammer between alarm bells. The shrink could have told her any number of things. Which comment did he choose for disclosure? Why now? My weekend plans were fading fast. Hands down, my mom had the greatest interviewing skills of all time. Of course, that's a 'bad thing' if you happen to be one of her kids. There was no getting away with anything.

"What're you talking about, Mom?" I asked

"Your therapist spent fifteen minutes telling me about your antics. You're not taking this seriously at all." She was firm: "Why are you doing this?"

"Doing what, Mom?"

"You know what you said." She began searching her purse for car keys while walking toward the parking lot. A bad time for my reticence, she looked at me and said, "He told me that you asked him, 'Do you actually get paid to do this?'"

"Mom, it's just a joke." I said.

"How about joking around after you get your anger figured out. Why aren't you talking to him honestly? Tell the therapist why you became so angry over these past two years? That's what we're coming here for."

She had tears in her eyes. I immediately slowed myself down. I didn't like to see her sad. I was unhappy to see that I was hurting my mother. Our usual bantering was only a ghostly presence inside the car. I remember the dry heat blowing through the dashboard vents and the dampened swish of car tires going through rainwater. The silence was unnerving. Her exhaustion was emotional and if I didn't figure something out, one of my four older siblings would surely twist my lips. My words would now need to somehow become profound. What I said next needed to show specificity and compassion.

"I don't know." I said.

"You don't know." She paused. "Well, if you're not going to tell this doctor, will you tell me?" she asked.

"Tell you what?" I knew my responses were weak. I was buying time to find an answer that she might accept.

"Never mind, Danny. If you can't see how your behavior is upsetting your father and me, then I'm beginning to think we have a bigger problem on our hands."

I needed to say something because that meant she was going to look into other options.

"What do you want me to say, Mom?" The avoidance tactic was used one last time.

"How about why you changed from being happy to angry? Or why you want to hurt other people even if it means hurting yourself in the process."

We came to a stop and I maintained eye contact until the reflecting traffic light on her face changed, red to green. She turned her attention back to the road and let the silence work on me a bit more. What I did not mention to her is that I actually enjoyed therapy. Somehow, I think she knew but chose not to sabotage any future treatments.

I agreed to give it a serious try with a new therapist so, of course, it didn't take long before she found one. Research and "word of mouth" found Buddy Portuge. This is where I began making changes. It was a completely different experience from the first one, not weighted down by constant agreement or filler phrases like "It seems like" and "How do you feel." When I sat down in Buddy's office, it was like talking to an old friend. I felt comfortable enough to talk about anything. He listened and asked questions before coming out with his preliminary assessment. At the time, he looked to be in his early forties. A little slang and a very relaxed posture made me wonder if he was once a flower child.

"Listen man," he said, scooting to the front of his chair. "Are you listening?"

"Sure, yeah." I looked away.

"I mean it. This is gonna be good. Listen to my words carefully," he said.

"I'm listening."

"You're passionate about helping the defenseless," he said.

"What's so earth-shattering about that? I'm not the only one that doesn't like to see people get kicked around," I snarled. "Take a look at punk culture. There's a ton of kids out there trying to salvage justice."

"It's up to you. I'm not saying you're a heroic type, if that's what you're thinking," he commented. "What I am saying is that you're letting emotion override intellect. More investment, you're going to need a broader menu if you're gonna do this kind of work. In this society where you're living, you'll need credibility to get people the help they need."

Buddy coaxed my participation by revealing just enough evidence to shake my indifference. He offered a canvas from which I could begin to mix and sort new colors. Unlike the other shrink, Buddy gathered information about the nature of my conduct issues.

"When you choose to put your body on the line with these guys that are twice your size, you'll get more than a butt kicking when you turn eighteen" he said.

"You mean jail or something?" I asked.

"Let's just say it'll be more than what you're currently willing to risk, like a bloody nose." Then he looked me straight in the eyes before inducing a healthy amount of guilt, "Keep in mind, any other unfortunate souls out there will miss out on getting the kind of help that your passion can potentially provide. You, my friend, could do some meaningful work in this world."

Boundaries, especially when aimed at my areas of weakness, helped to motivate me. He had a respectful manner, tactful at framing a deficit. He listened to my philosophical vomit until he felt he had enough to build a tailored template.

I began making serious choices for myself at the age of seventeen. I started to see education in a different way. I grew closer to the idea of college after seeing it from a new perspective. Insight, maturity, desperation, luck whatever...change began to occur rapidly. I even surrendered, not conformed, to the idea of personal presentation. I cut my hair and went with "smile and the world smiles back." Or, as my Mom says, "Make sure you brush your teeth and speak clearly—no ahs and ums."

Buddy pointed out how my years of exposure to a close friend going through physical and psychological abuse had an impact on my thoughts and behavior. I became hyper-vigilant to a victim's cry for help. I decided to change my attitude about how I could approach the problem. Until this time, I was operating from broad generalizations. I associated college with corporate affluence and ungratefulness. I trusted adults less after witnessing abuse in the homes of my close friends. People looked more and more apathetic as they aged and they all seemed to follow a cult-like phenomenon. It was like bugs drawn to light when it came to adults and their decisions involving money. But all of these childhood experiences helped me decide how I wanted to spend my adult work life.

In just a few months, I felt good about letting myself grow up. I took interest in what motivated human behavior instead of impulsively confronting it. I became convinced that I had a better chance of helping people through a professional path. I earned my undergraduate degree in Psychology then a Masters in Social Work. My first ten years of employment was in a medical treatment model. It's fulfilling to work as a team with nurses, psychiatrists, pediatricians, counselors, speech therapists, occupational therapists, school teachers, and law enforcement. Consultation is easily accessed and treatment plans are very thorough.

In 1999, I was presented with having to decide whether to relocate or begin a private practice. At the time, I was on the child mental health team with a local HMO. The medical group was forced to leave the health care market at the same time that state mental health reform was pushing service delivery from county to community. Private practice began to feel less intimidating the group allowing me to take my existing caseload and pediatricians assuring referrals from their own newly established clinics. Irony struck and I became the entrepreneur "prep" that I had once made fun of as a teenager.

The Reform in 1999 created high demand for a community based child mental health clinic and in 2000, I opened my own pediatric clinic. By 2004, referral demands generated enough work for six clinicians and two support staff. I had prepared clinic operations to meet the state's local reform and made provider access a priority. All insurances were accepted, including Medicaid. Running the business was time intensive and my role quickly became divided between administrative and clinical responsibilities. Unfortunately, a culmination of events led to the closing at the end of 2005. A major deciding factor, as you will read, is at the intersection of law and ethics.

I. The Initial Interview

I waited for traffic to clear before crossing with a full cup of coffee. The morning routine started with Mark, my business coordinator. Mark was the "ears and eyes" of clinic operations. His vantage point allowed for the occasional "heads up" when potential hazards were attached to a case. Parents took care of business matters in his office. Mark and I built custom doors, split in half with counter tops at chest level. This way, parents could check in with support staff and schedule appointments while partitioning kids off from therapy offices in the back.

The lobby had a soothing beach mural. A bucket, sand covered shovel, flip flops and scattered shells helped keep the calm. I kept my eyes on the scene even after closing the first custom door behind me. Following a slurp off the surface, I walked several feet and then placed my coffee cup on the shelf of the second one.

"Today's the day" Mark said.

"Who referred this one?" I asked.

"DSS," he said. "The dad's been calling every other day to see if you've had any cancellations. He says Dr. Shaffer and Dr. Fontaine highly recommended you." Mark put his hands next to his face and wiggled his fingers. "Ooooh. Now you have the DSS doctors referring to you. I'll try to keep up."

He pointed at a couple of charts stacked on the counter beside my arm.

"Hip-itty hop," he looked at his watch, "your admirer is showing up in about eight minutes. Don't think about having any phone time because he's had paperwork completed for nearly five weeks."

I picked up my stack of charts and bantered, "Thanks for nothing." I made only a few steps toward my office and Mark made an addendum.

"One other thing, he's got Tagna insurance. There's something screwy about it though, because I can't get an authorization."

Before seeing a new patient, we tried to iron out any potential insurance snags. Most of the time, it was an understood responsibility of the provider to call the insurance to attain an authorization number. If we didn't have authorization by the time of the initial visit, payment wasn't promised.

"So, what's the deal? Is he paying out of pocket today?" I asked.

"I don't know yet. It might be through his Employee Assistance Program. I'll call Tagna and try to have it figured out by the time you're out of session." Mark said.

I heard the beep of the lobby door. I put my charts down on the desk and then slowly inhaled steam from my coffee cup. I took a short moment to gaze at the morning traffic below my window. After a few stretches, I walked down to the lobby.

I approached a seated couple and extended my right hand, "Good morning. I'm Danny Dawson, are you Mr. Schultz?"

"Yes, I'm Joe." He stood to shake my hand and I couldn't help noticing his rigid posture.

Then to the lady standing beside him, I again extended my right hand. "Hi, I'm Danny. You are...?"

"I'm Diane." she replied.

"Nice to meet both of you. Follow me back to my office and we'll get started."

Small talk was a staple in these first meetings but I chose to make chit-chat about the insurance problem.

"We're still working on the authorization from Tagna but we'll get that worked out. Have you used your mental health benefit in the past?" I asked.

"No."

There wasn't going to be any chit chat as long as the answers were that short. People can sometimes leave you hanging off a cliff, like Wiley Coyote. It makes conversation tough when the ground isn't solid. Walking behind me, they couldn't see my eyes widen and my lips take whistle form. I stopped at the threshold and motioned them to enter my office ahead of me. Joe and Diane chose to sit on the couch and I sat in one of the lazy boy chairs across from them.

"Bear with me this first go around while I ask a bunch of questions." Darting the paper with my pen I added, "Don't hesitate to interrupt me if there's something that comes to mind or something you'd like to add," I explained.

Joe was an average build but a bit overweight. Both were casually dressed and appeared about forty years old. Joe had short black hair that looked like it could have been cut with a straight edge with the front bangs way up at the scalp. He had rose-colored cheeks, wide eyes, and a small mouth. One side of his mouth deviated from the hairstyle with a slight upward curve. For some crazy reason, he was starting to remind me of Lady Elaine Fairchild from "Mr. Rogers Neighborhood." I don't think the show had implications suggesting the same for Lady Elaine, but this character was ringing the "spectrum bell."

"So, let me listen a little bit about what's going on currently and what you'd like to see accomplished from therapy before I get into my list of history questions," I prompted.

Suddenly a stack of papers appeared from Joe's hand. Each time I made eye contact with Diane, she reacted with a quick smile and seat adjustment.

"You should just have your office manager make copies of these," he shook the stack. "It'll tell you the whole story."

Condescending folks are no fun at all. Boundaries obviously needed more definition.

"Those look like court orders. Am I right?" I asked.

"Yeah. But this paper tells the whole history in a timeline sequence" he said.

I began making statements that were intended to convey my role relative to the treatment he expected.

"I'll be glad to look over that timeline sheet but not the orders just yet."

Joe handed the single sheet of paper to me and rested the court orders in his lap. The line item sheet had a bunch of topics related to family and residences. One of the lines read "Joe and Diane got married".

Looking at Diane, I asked "Are you Sherry's biological mother?"

3

The little smile and readjustment was followed by a hot potato look of deferment over to Joe. Poor thing was looking for clearance, I guess.

Joe took the wheel on her behalf, "If you read on, you'll see that her real mom is in a lot of trouble. We've been at this for a long time. Sherry wasn't cared for," he said.

I presumed Diane's answer was "No."

"Are there specific behavioral problems she's having?"

"She's well behaved," Joe was trying to pick up the pace of the interview. "She's just scared to death when it comes time to go back to her mother's house. She'll wet herself mostly and sometimes...you know...."

"...soil herself," Diane locked on.

"Yeah. Her mom is totally unreliable. What can you expect from someone who marries a violent criminal?"

Diane put her hand on Joe's knee and quietly said, "Be sure to mention the school issues."

Joe responded to her with a tight smile of approval. "Sherry's attendance record, from when she lived with her mom, was really bad. Sherry basically went to school when her mom got up on time and when she felt like bringing her," he said.

"What's bio mom's name." I asked.

"What?" Joe asked

I stopped to look up from documenting. "What's Sherry's biological mom's name?"

"June." He answered.

It felt as if someone flipped a switch on a movie projector. The air changed as the tempo slipped into a sluggish cadence. I'm sure my jaw was open slightly as my head ping-ponged between them.

"Is it the same last name as Sherry's? What was that, Gill..." prompting Joe to complete the correct spelling.

Reluctantly, Joe confirmed "G-I-L-L-A-N-D."

When sensitive information is disclosed, I freeze the moment in a way that etches the reporter's memory. That makes it easier for the person to reference should there be any conflict with information received in future reports. The best way to do that is to first get the person to completely verbalize the information. Assist them but avoid contaminating their vocabulary preferences. Key words and phrases helped to establish reference points in future conversations. There's less chance of misinterpretation or reason to perceive a presence of bias on the part of the health care provider. Subtleties in language can be most helpful in a clinical review. Fair is fair. All cards must be played face up if we're working for the child's best interest.

"So, where's she living?" I continued.

"She's one county over, in Deer" Joe said.

"Is it okay to go ahead and talk about family history so I can understand how she came to have a different last name than yours, Joe?"

There was a long pause while Joe and Diane sat motionless on the sofa. I began scribbling a couple squares and circles for a geneogram.

"You and June were never married?" I asked Joe.

"No. I didn't even know Sherry existed until she was four years old," he said. "That's what I'm trying to tell you, she didn't even tell me about her until she found a way to make money off of it for herself." He was miffed about something.

I was trying to think if I had missed something he said earlier about Sherry's mom.

"You're saying that June, Sherry's mom, didn't tell you about Sherry until she was four years old?" I was expressing myself in a much more sympathetic manner. Keep the emotion fresh and hope for details.

Diane found an opening and took a risk, "It's just sick, absolutely sick. This child is beautiful and I, for the life of me, have no idea how any person could do some of the things that this woman has done."

I could feel Joe's affirmation. I wanted to grab a bunch of construction paper and write separate numbers like: 8.5, 9.8, and 10.0. "Here, Joe, just select one of these and hold it above your head after each time your wife says something.

"For starters she WAS, and I emphasize WAS, married to a criminal. Thankfully, it looks like she's finally gonna start following the court orders."

I didn't think his wide-eyed shark stare would ever break but he looked over at Diane before continuing, "I have full custody rights and Sherry is now going to a private catholic school. Everything about her has changed since she started living with me…and Diane."

I tried to keep the interview focused, "Can you tell me how DSS got involved?"

"Skip Gilland basically went on some kind of rampage and was thrown in a state mental hospital. When he got out he started stalking June and I don't know if he forced himself on her or what but they ended up back together like Bonnie and Clyde. They couldn't accept the paternity test and they'd try to keep Sherry from me. My attorney is no idiot. She was like, "Just give it time, he'll do something stupid again." Sure enough, he did. He called DSS and reported me for sexually abusing Sherry," Joe said.

I was moving my head back and forth in a "Gee, that's too bad" motion. "That must've been a long process. I mean, in terms of the interviewing and medical appointments."

Joe replied, "It just keeps all of this at a standstill. Sherry needs to talk about her feelings and just be able to be a kid. She doesn't need any more interference. She's had enough." Joe added.

Since DSS was involved, a caseworker or someone would likely want verification of treatment at some point. So I asked him for information about the assigned social worker. "I can call if you have the name of the person."

Joe obviously had a position on this matter as well.

"Any communication has to go through my attorney first. Actually, she may want to talk with you even before you meet Sherry," Joe directed.

"Your attorney?" I asked.

"Darla Tennor." Pointing at the initial paperwork, "I put all her information in there."

Again, if for no reason other than to reinforce who would be calling the plays, I chose to exercise the limits of our relationship.

"Unless there are imminent circumstances, it would definitely be in the best interest of Sherry if I avoid any communication until after the first few meetings."

Joe shrugged his shoulders as if it wasn't a big deal but he couldn't hide the fire engine-red that came over his face. "Darla worked hard with the parent coordinator to get all of this in place, that's all I'm say'n."

"I'm hearing more and more about parent coordinators. Did this person work with Sherry?" I asked.

"No," he spiked.

"Are you continuing to see the parent coordinator?"

"Sherry's mom doesn't go. Keep in mind it's in the court order."

It was beginning to become branded in my mind, thank you.

"So, there isn't a parent coordinator right now?" I clarified.

"She couldn't afford it." Diane felt obligated to make an addendum after Joe winced at her. "So she says, but we all know that's not the real issue."

Moving right along….

I interjected, "And what's this guy's name by the way? I think you mentioned it just a moment ago."

"Skip," Joe answered.

"Skip…" again, leading for a last name, Joe just stared through me.

Diane, however, was postured like a student in the front row, poised to participate.

"She lived with them for the first four years of her life," she said.

Joe moved his head like a bird. Glaring at her, he squawked "We don't know that."

Diane looked down at her feet. Bad, Diane.

He kept coloring the canvas with information about Skip but what I wanted was some kind of clue as to whether Skip was still married to Sherry's mom.

""The whole time Sherry was with them it was filled with fighting and separation," Joe's tone was getting more and more gritty. "I mean, come on, this guy carries a gun practically everywhere he goes and he's a drug user. He's been arrested for a bunch of different stuff. He's got at least one DWI and there's plenty of witnesses that say he is violent."

Here was another opportunity for a vocabulary etching.

"The word violent is pretty scary stuff when we're talking about someone as young as Sherry." I paused and placed my pad of paper down for a moment. "What kind of exposures do you think Sherry may've had while living with Skip and June? I'm going under the assumption they were under the same roof for a period of time, right?"

Diane looked at Joe and said, "Sherry must have been there when the police came and arrested Gilland, right?"

There's that name again.

"Diane? I'm sorry to cut in. What was that name you just said? Is that Skip's last name as well? Gilland?"

"Yes. Gilland. Same spelling, G-I-L-L-A-N-D...." Joe's eye brows went down.

Nice. Where would I be if not for Diane's assistance?

Joe kept the same slight curve on one side of his mouth. I remember thinking it was peculiar but the shark stare was the thing that put spirals in my eyes.

Joe didn't like the fact that the information was important enough for me to reach for my note pad again.

"Yeah, but read the information because the paternity test is done and that's all there is to it. It was 99.99999 something. I think that's proof enough."

That was an interesting and timely comment, Mr. Schultz.

"June herself took papers on Skip. She had him arrested because he violated a restraining order she took out on him. There's something in there about assault because he punched a teenage kid in the face," Joe dictated.

"Holy cow! What's that all about? Was Sherry around to see this?"

"I'm sure she was because it was June's son that he punched out," Joe said.

"June has a teenage son? Is this child from a different relationship?" I asked.

This time, it was Joe seeking confirmation from Diane. She was again at the front of her seat, in motion and ready to take the baton.

"There are actually two teenage sons that she has. Both of them are from June's previous marriage.

Now, we're getting somewhere.

Let's review: my patient is an eight year old girl with two half-brothers, teenagers from biological mother's first marriage. After divorcing, she married Mr. Gilland. We still don't know how Sherry and the people sitting in front of me ended up in the same house. I can only work with what they are willing to give to me…right?

"So, then, June is divorced from her first husband and now divorced from her second husband? Is that correct?" A drum roll sounds.

While Diane was obviously more tuned into family history than Joe, this one seemed to stump both of them.

"I don't know if they're married or not."

"And the two of you are married, correct?" I asked

"Yes" Joe answered

"How long have you been married?"

"We just got married not too long ago."

Clear enough, I guess. He didn't like family talk for some reason.

"What about extended family? Sherry's Grandparents, are they nearby?" I asked Joe.

"No." He snapped.

I don't think Diane knew when to quit either because she seemed motivated to answer more questions. She looked at Joe and said, "There's my mother. She's here in Hoffman County."

That conversation lasted another thirty seconds before we were back to silence. We talked about Sherry's relationship with Diane's mother but there wasn't any information offered about June's parents. I decided to move on and get this info from bio mom. IF I get to meet bio mom, that is.

"Let's go through any of the developmental information you may have. Do you know if she was using any substances during pregnancy—smoking or…." I was interrupted by Joe.

"Seriously, what does this have to do with the therapy? She's gonna talk to you and draw some pictures, right? I'm just say'n, we didn't have to go through all this before."

Say again?

"She was in treatment before DSS got involved?" I asked.

Joe sighed. He was putting forth effort to inhibit himself at this point.

"She didn't see anyone long enough to even mention ..." he paused. Those wide eyes kept looking out the window as if he were witnessing a shuttle launch.

"I'd rather my attorney talk with you," his focus whiplashed "before I provide you with too much more information".

I had my doubts about the willingness of an attorney to act like a "treatment team member." His comfort level was pushed far enough because our conversation abruptly concluded.

Joe stood up and ushered Diane toward the door. It sort of felt like he may not want to return but he firmed things up with the comment, "We'll have Sherry with us at the next meeting—see you then."

Note to self: control is relative.

II. I Can't Talk About Daddy Or Mommy'll Go to Jail

S herry stood with her back flat against the wall in the lobby. She held her arms in a "T" position and was bending at the waist back and forth. I recognized Joe but he was on the other side of the lobby. Sherry stood closer to a lady and her son who were waiting for a different therapist.

"Hi, Sherry, I'm Danny."

Fine black hair outlined Sherry's fair skinned face.

"Hi," Sherry replied.

"If it's okay with your Dad and if it's okay with you, I'd like you to come back and do a little talk'n and a little play'n at the same time. You've done that before, right?" I made a sort of nutty face and her laughter helped break some ice.

"Yeah, okay," she said.

I looked over at Joe to give a thumbs-up as she ran past us. A child's first impression is big. I usually tell a silly story or other times; especially at the end of the week, I'll just place something on top of my head. Business as usual, there's just something on my head. It's tough for kids to open up, especially in split loyalty matters. It becomes easier after areas of sensitivity are fully surveyed. I try for a casual presentation, paying close attention to the action-reaction concept. Indifference on delicate topics is an absolute law of mine—no matter what.

I sat down with Sherry and started to draw a family tree.

"Squares will be boys and circles will be girls." I explained.

I drew a square and a circle, representing Joe and Diane. Pointing in the direction of the lobby, I asked "You called him...."

"Joe" she said. She got up quickly after her colored pencil rolled off the table. "But, he's NOT my Dad."

Mindful of any reaction, I moved forward by looking back to the paper right away.

"Joe or Joseph?"

Sherry shrugged her shoulders.

"That's fine." Pointing at the circle now "And her name is Diane, right?" I asked.

"Yeah." Her face sort of relaxed.

I drew another circle representing her mother.

"And this right here is your…."

She interrupted with an abrupt hand crashing into the bin of colored markers.

"I'll draw Mommy," she said.

"Very cool. Go right ahead," I encouraged.

She made a neat little stick figure with long brown hair. I tapped my finger on the paper next to where she drew mommy.

"Maybe I'm wrong, but I'm trying to remember if…." I paused, mindful of how she wanted me to refer to him.

Sherry looked up from her paper with a knuckle sandwhich stare. That was clearly her way of telling me not to screw it up.

"Joe." I said.

"Okay, then. I thought I remember him saying your mom *was* or maybe *is* married to…."

Sherry scooted her chair back and put her hands over her mouth.

In a muffled voice, she said, "I can't talk about Daddy or mommy'll go to jail."

The family tree was facing Sherry. I put my index fingers on two points of the paper and spun it 180 degrees.

"Okay. No talking about him." I watched Sherry peripherally as I drew a square next to June. We both understood this square belonged to Daddy. She had stopped to watch my pencil. In that moment, a cold fear smoked through the vents of my office. She nibbled at the sides of her cheek while carrying on with a campfire stare.

Just as every other circle and square had a name, so did this one. I wrote "Daddy"—she tried to hide a smile but went straight back to her doodling. I loosened up a bit. She seemed comfortable with my decision.

She changed the topic. "What's your favorite color?"

I took one final risk "Wait, wait, wait." Again pointing at Daddy's square and then over to Joe's square, I asked, "If Joe and Diane say it's okay, can we talk about him then?"

Her head went back and forth for about twenty seconds. "No," she said.

I looked up and squinted. "Oh, man, I get it. That's probably why you're mostly in this house now, right?"

She continued drawing. "It's not because he's bad, like they say. He's nice," she said.

"What do you mean?" I picked myself up and walked to the pencil sharpener.

"He's nice, he's not mean," she said.

I took my time at the pencil sharpener. I started doing an up and down squatting motion.

"Well, how long have you known him?" I asked.

Sherry was definitely entertained by my weird movements. She had a huge smile on her face.

"He's my *Daddy*. He's been with me forever, silly man" she said.

Still sharpening, I added a side kick at the top of my squat.

"That makes sense, huh? Mommy and Daddy. But what about when you were itzy witzy diaper walk'n baby?" I asked.

She let out some laughter and suddenly stood up next to her chair. Kids can get in a trance. It's similar to watching TV and someone tries encroaching. Most of the time, kids will understand what you're saying but the trance is way more important to them. Sherry kept right on talking. It was an uncomfortable topic but she was zoned in with a big smile.

"Duhhhhh," her face scrunched. "I have pictures of me and him when I was just born."

Something wasn't matching up. I played for a while longer before I mentioned it would soon be time for me to get Joe to join us. She started a slow, anxious gallop around perimeter of my office.

"Then I'm hiding" she said.

She rolled my office chair back and then crawled under my desk. That kind of behavior wasn't something I saw too much. My curiousity was growing by the minute.

13

"Hey? What's the deal?" I asked.

"Be quiet. Don't tell him I'm here. Tell him I'm in a different room. I want to hear what he says about my mommy," she said.

"*What?*"

"Schultz lies," she said.

I hadn't heard her refer to Joe by his last name until then.

"Schultz? That's his last name?" I said.

"Yeah, so?" she snapped.

She was different all of a sudden.

"Wait a second." I said "You think he's going to talk nasty about your Mommy?"

She pulled the office chair closer to her crawled up body.

"He lies all the time. He hates my mommy." I saw small pools balancing on the edge of her eyelids when she added, "I want to go home."

"Home? At Mommy's home?" I asked.

"Yeah." The tears streamed down her face. She took the tissues I offered but she was too frustrated and just held them against her forehead. "I hate my new school and I *hate* him," she said.

I sat down on the carpet floor and said nothing for a minute or two. We were making absolutely no movement; nothing could be heard but the sound of the second hand on my office clock.

"Sherry? I want to ask you something and I want you to really think about it before you answer, okay?" My tone was soft but more serious than she'd heard from me to this point.

I continued with important questions having to do with her safety. She was denying any lethality or abuse but maintained an overall sadness and insecurity about living with Joe Schultz.

"If you're wondering if he might say something…." I started.

"You mean, lie. He lies about her. He lies about everything," she said. "Did he tell you about the blood test?" she asked.

Wow, somebody sat and tried to explain the paternity test to her.

"What did the blood test say?"

"It says that he's my real dad. Guess what? It would say Daddy's my real dad if they'd let me spend more time with him. I NEVER get to see him." The beads of tears ran closer together but her eyes widened with frustration.

All I could do at this moment was to stay present. I didn't have any answer for her and not enough information to encourage any sort of hope that she could rely on as far as a return home to her mommy, daddy, and two step brothers.

"How much longer until you get to make a decision about where I get to live?" she asked.

"Me?"

"Yeah. The court yard, where you can tell them where I want to live."

After a deep breath, I approached her "Sherry. I want to help," I said.

Her hands were locked around the base of the chair. Thankfully, she loosened her grip after I gave a slight tug.

"Why won't he just let me go home?" she asked. "It's like anything that I tell him…that I want to see Mommy and Daddy he just tells me it's not going to happen. Like it's never going to be the same," she said.

"I need to learn more about why you can't live with your mommy. I'll try to talk to different people and try to …"

KNOCK, KNOCK, KNOCK on my office door.

Her eyelids had just started to relax but jolted right back to a fear-widened stare. I looked at her and said, "I'm going to do my best. I'm not going to do anything that will get you in trouble."

Standing up from my squat position, I started toward the door. The delay must have made Schultz uneasy because he proceeded to open the door and walk right into the office.

"What's the verdict in here," Schultz asked.

I welcomed the entrance. "Come in, come in. She did wonderful…."

While I spoke with Schultz, Sherry slowly crawled out from under the desk. He didn't comment on her being under there and I wasn't about to enter into a discussion about it. She was watching me closely.

I looked at Mr. Schultz and then back at Sherry.

"Hey, could you remind me what the format was with her previous therapist?"

Schultz reached into his front pocket and took out his car keys.

"Same kind of deal," he said.

I think I understood him but thought the clarification wouldn't hurt.

"You mean like this, where she met individually with the therapist?"

He was unresponsive so I gave him an alternative.

"Or did you also have opportunity for family sessions where both biological parents would meet with the therapist."

There was a slight rise in the right corner of his coin-slot sized mouth. There's something Stephen King-ish about this guy. He wanted too many things kept quiet, particularly concerning the avoidance of previous treatment. His pace of distraction took a different form when he began to bark out commands to Sherry.

"Pick up the markers and paper. Diane's waiting for us in the car."

I smiled and stepped closer, making eye contact. "I'm real interested in trying to get biological parents together, if it's possible," I held my breath.

"No. We're not here for mediation or family counseling," he said.

"I understand," I paused to side-step Mr. Schultz so that I could see Sherry. I squinted between my thumb and index finger and said to her, "I know you have to go so I'll make this really short."

Sherry didn't hesitate. It was as if we had rehearsed this moment. She stood up from the small table and pointed toward the lobby "I'll wait out there."

"Joe, she's under the impression that if she talks about certain people in her family that her mom will end up in jail."

As if to say, "Maybe it's true" his only response was a shoulder shrug.

"It's co-parenting that's gonna help with these adjustment related symptoms, Joe."

"Co-parenting?" his tone and posture were condescending. "I'm saying we don't need mediation. Judge Klein wants Sherry to have her own therapist to talk with. I'd ask her about whether you should be encouraging Sherry to talk about people that break the law."

Why was it necessary to wag authority? Who was ultimately going to write this treatment plan, Judge Klein? I could only try to continue to somehow get his brain to see that Sherry's needs included access to attachment figures.

"Joe, I'm not talking about you and June coming in my office to divide up days of the year for visitation. What I do is assess and then provide suggestions to improve functioning. There are some attachment issues at the core of this for Sherry. The quality of a long term bond with yourself can suffer if she perceives that you're controlling her relationship with her mother."

"I'm not controlling anything, it's the law that her mother is dealing with. That's probably something at some point you'll need to talk with Sherry about," he said.

"What's that?" I asked.

"The adjustment of having a mom that can't seem to follow rules," he snapped back.

I cocked my head a little side-ways and looked up for just a moment. He kept at it for a little longer.

"You've gotta admit, when she finally understands that her mom is at fault for all of these sudden changes, it's gonna be hard."

That's quite a reach for him when he tries to communicate anything having to do with compassion. His face sort of strains naturally, like puckering from the sour taste of a lemon.

He was on a disclosure roll so I postured myself as the interested audience.

"I hate to even send her over there because she's gotta lay in filth. She has to sleep on a pallet with a sheet on it and deal with bugs all around her. And who knows how many men Sherry sees coming in and out of June's place," he scowled.

"Whoa. She hasn't mentioned anything like that. Are you sure?" I asked.

"There's a lot you don't know about this woman and the way she treats Sherry. When do you think she ever brought her to get her teeth looked at by a dentist? I'm having to pay for all these mistakes and there's no way June's getting back involved…too late for that."

Given there seemed to be a lot more to the picture, I put in a word for continuity's sake.

"At what point can I get together and talk with her, then?" I was maintaining eye contact as best I could "because it makes a world of difference when primary attachment figures are at least given opportunity to participate."

"Listen," he stretched his hands above his head, "good luck trying to get her to keep an appointment. She won't pay even if she does show up," pausing for a quick breath, "and I don't want you billing any sessions against Sherry's insurance visits. You can't do that."

Something told me he knew more about the insurance than he was leading us to believe but I can let that sit for another moment or two.

Good enough for me at the moment. At least I had given both he and Sherry a message that I was interested in June's participation. Joe had a message for me as well and it wasn't favorable.

Before they left, I walked out to the lobby to say good-bye to Sherry. The hug and smile she gave to me before leaving communicated a passing grade on my first test of trust.

III. Tell the Tooth

As I've explained, families normally check in with Mark and then wait in the lobby for their therapist. I was in my office talking with a school counselor when there was a knock at my office door. Thinking it was Mark alerting me of Sherry's arrival, I continued the telephone conversation while opening my door.

Tethered close to Mr. Shultz, Sherry looked weepy and exhausted. With dry lips and a mouthful of cotton balls, she obviously had a visit with the dentist.

With the phone still to my ear, Joe said "I guess she'll be drawing for you today because she can't talk."

Luckily, Mark came sliding around the corner, "Hi, Sherry, hi, Mr. Schultz."

While eye contact appeared tough most times, Mr. Schultz seemed locked onto mine at the moment. Sherry attended to Mark by turning her head to him but Mr. Schultz refused to acknowledge him.

Mark coaxed them to follow him back to the lobby but I ended my conversation with the school counselor right away. And after hanging up the phone, I crouched down beside Sherry with my hand placed on her shoulder.

"You look tuckered out, Sherry."

A slow affirming nod and grimacing expression told the story.

"Looks like a dentist thing, am I right?" I asked.

Another affirming nod accompanied by pointing inside her mouth.

"Say 'I just had two cavities filled,'" Joe offered on her behalf.

Schultz looked eager to get inside my office.

"So," he said, "did you get a hold of June?"

"You know what?" I stood up "...glad you're remembering, I didn't see June's contact information in the initial paperwork."

Schultz's eyes lids lowered, maybe the enema kicked in. A simple shrug communicated a strong disinterred for bringing any convenience to this process of information gathering.

"I can get up with you about it later. Sherry probably would like to crawl in the sheets and rest her face rather than talk with me right now, don't you think?"

Sherry looked relieved. Rest was definitely the ticket for her right now.

"You can draw some pictures," Joe repeated.

Sherry's eyes closed and she leaned against the wall outside of my office.

"Sherry!" Schultz pulled her back to position. "You need your therapy."

With hands on her shoulders, Schultz turned her about face to lean her over the office threshold.

I walked Sherry over to the couch where she collapsed without hesitation.

With her eyes closed, she began to whisper.

"Sherry," I quietly interrupted, "I don't know if I'll be able to understand you. I'm sorry."

Her eyes moved under the lids before opening. She was so tired. Sherry pointed to my scratch paper and colored pencils lying on the table.

"Are you sure you want that, right now?" I asked.

She nodded her head. I gave her a clipboard and offered a few pencils from the bin but she only wanted one.

"I get it: You just want to write something down."

After a short time, she dropped the clipboard on the floor and returned to shut eye mode.

I reached down and turned the clipboard over to read the writing:

He won't let me talk to Mommy

I was quiet in my response. "You have scheduled times to talk with Mommy, right?" I reminded her.

A small tear ran from a wincing set of closed eyes before sitting up to write again:

Schultz is mean.

She had told me about how much she looked forward to talking with her mom in the evening. They talked and watched their favorite TV show together. Even though it wasn't as good as when she watched it with her mommy and daddy and brothers, she could at least laugh over the telephone. Sherry and June apparently chose the time for that very reason.

"What about the TV show time you told me about?

He listened on the fone. Mommy and me laft to loud he is mean about us lafing.

Another pattern in these custody cases are vindictive acts by one parent that sabotage the child's relationship with the other parent.

"You know, I've been wondering how I can get in touch with your mommy," I said.

Without hesitation, she wrote it down on the paper.

"Okay, got it," my voice cracked with emotion.

She grimaced in pain but seemed content when her eyes were closed. I decided to see if I could persuade Joe to take her home.

"I'm gonna see if I can talk to your…" I stopped myself this time "…him and see if he's ok with taking you home early so you can go to bed. Sound good?"

With her eyes closed, she nodded.

"I'll be right back," I said.

I found Joe in Mark's office. They were discussing the insurance problem.

"Joe, can I talk with you for just a moment?" I asked.

"We're talking about money," Joe announced. "I'm sure you want to get paid, don't you?"

"Getting paid, I've learned, is an important thing," I acknowledged, "but can you just give me a minute across the hall?"

His fixed smile was getting to me. For nearly a minute, I was in a staring contest with him. I forfeited.

"How 'bout it?" I coaxed.

Reluctantly, he followed me across the hall to an open office.

"Joe, I'd strongly recommend bringing her home so she can rest. She's really uncomfortable back there," I said.

The smile vanished.

"You can't charge me. You know that, right? This is YOUR recommendation, not mine," he turned to exit the office before adding an emphatic "Don't forget you're the one that cancelled the appointment."

His pace was heavy as he walked to office. I followed closely to observe whatever came next.

He opened my office door, "Let's go, Sherry." She was dreamy-eyed as he strong-armed her up off the sofa. "Excuse us," he sidestepped past me.

They were gone, down the hall and out the door. I watched Joe and Sherry get into their car and drive away.

All jokes aside, this man has an illness.

Mark came sliding into the lobby, "I was on the phone two minutes, he didn't leave, did he?"

"Joe? Yeah, he's gone," I said.

Mark was leaning his forehead against a window overlooking the parking lot. His head pivoted for a panoramic view, hoping to spot them.

He waved me off in frustration, "Damn it."

Mark's motivation was all about having an empty inbox. Payment delays burned up stomach acid and kept him pacing. All he could do was shake his head before starting back to his office.

"What's the deal? What did you want him for, his copay?"

I thought I saw a slow stream of smoke coming from his ears.

"Listen, man, we've not received any payment from his insurance yet."

"What's the hold up?" I asked.

"Tagna insurance outsources the mental health benefit to a company called Social Well. They're based out of Chicago." Mark sat down on the arm of a lobby sofa. "I'm telling you, the credentialing process with this place is like no other," he said.

"Is there something we still need him to do in order to get it straight?"

"I need his signature for the release. Right now it says 'Tagna' and I need a release specifying this outsourced company on it." Mark looked plenty upset. "He knew I needed his signature before leaving. I swear, it's like he's intentionally dragging his feet at this point." He gave his head a rough scratch and added, "There's something amiss with him. I'm telling you, the guy's got some wicked ways about him."

"So, is he giving us a copayment or anything?" I asked.

"He's been paying a twenty dollars copay." Mark leaned forward, "But here's a twist: his copay amount with SocialWell is only 6.60 dollars."

"What a bizarre amount," I replied.

"What's bizarre," Mark added, "is that he keeps paying us twenty when he's known about the outsourcing company and that he only needs to pay 6.60."

Was this mental illness, manipulation, or both? This was getting more screwy by the minute.

IV. Silly Man Decides If I Get To Come Home

With Sherry's help, I managed to arrange a meeting with June. My preference was to meet with her individually but her work wasn't allowing much flexibility. She informed me that a great deal of time had already been used to attend court hearings and that any further time off could result in job loss. So we met on her scheduled visitation day with Sherry.

"Are you June?" I asked.

Sherry was like a jumping bean. She was doing twirls in the middle of the lobby, busting with excitement.

"I am she. And are you silly man?" she laughed.

"I am he. It's nice to meet you, Mom."

June struck me from the beginning as a warm and authentic person. She picked up her black purse, placed it over her shoulder and then crouched down to pick up her coffee cup.

"Hope you don't mind," pointing at her cup, "it's a bad habit but if I quit right now it wouldn't be good. Trust me," she laughed.

After getting settled in the office, I cupped my hands around my mouth and then scooted to the edge of my seat.

"So, what can you tell me about this wonderful girl you have here, Ms. Gilland?"

Sherry's smiling face appeared from behind the lower left side of June's chair. June joined right in and hollered back with cupped hands in place.

"Oh. Let me think. Umm…umm…. There must be something good to say about her. Hmmm, there must be something…I'm still thinking…."

Like a pop-it toy, Sherry jumped out from behind the chair with her hands on her hips.

"Hey!" she protested.

June reeled her in to embrace her. They hugged quietly in this moment together. Their bond was natural and soothing.

I continued, "She really looks forward to visits with you, June. What's your secret sauce? What do the two of you usually do together?"

June had a smile on her face. With her eyes on Sherry, she responded, "Not really much of anything, right? Just lots of goofing around. It's a short amount of time but we do the best we can with it, right?"

Sherry giggled after June gave her the 'zap' when you push on either side of someone's waist.

She added, "Sherry probably told you about her brothers, Tim and Rich, right?"

Sherry quickly turned and placed her hand over June's mouth.

"*Don't,*" she whispered to June.

June looked at Sherry then looked at me. Her voice became quite serious.

"Tim and Rich are your brothers, honey. They've known you your whole life. It's okay to talk about them."

Sherry was trying to undo a knot in her shoe lace. She looked up through a small stream of hair that fell forward. "But I've known Daddy all my life, too," she said.

June had a look of embarrassment. She leaned down to help Sherry with her shoe but was addressing me.

"You know they're from a completely different marriage, right?"

"Yes," I said.

"I know you probably think I'm some kind of...."

I interrupted her, "I'm not thinking anything, June."

June looked at me without expression – just stared for a moment as if she were looking at a mirage.

I repeated myself, "Really, I'm not thinking anything. Can you believe they pay me to observe beautiful moments like this. I am so lucky, don't you think?"

I looked over to Sherry, "Maybe someday you'll be working with kids and you can do this job for me."

I sat in a medium-sized lazy boy and draped my arms over the sides pretending it was a wheelchair.

In an old man voice, I said, "Maybe, help my grandkids learn how to deal with a crabby ol gran pappy."

Sherry started in on some toys that provided a sound screen.

"Did Joe tell you about the court orders and all the stuff about my husband?" she asked.

"Joe did inform me about him a bit. His name is Skip, correct?" I asked.

"Yeah. Same last name, Gilland."

June stood up and walked over to Sherry.

"Honey, Mommy's gonna talk a little bit with Mr. Dawson. I want you to play a little further over here so he and I can hear each other talk."

"I'll be more quiet," Sherry offered.

June was both firm and loving in her directives with Sherry.

"You're so nice to say that but I prefer you play a little further away from our discussion."

In the process of her persuasiveness, June had transferred play items to the new designated play spot. Sherry transferred easily and resumed her play.

"Here's the thing," June said, "the court has ordered me to keep Sherry away from Skip."

I had a puzzled look on my face.

"Well, by the sounds of it, Skip's had some problems with the law. Is that true?" I clarified.

June lowered her eyebrows, "So, what've you heard?"

I cleared my throat and said the following with emphasis: "It would be best to hear *your* version, June."

June rolled her eyes, looking somewhat disgusted.

"Have you talked with Darla Tenor?" referring to Joe's attorney.

"Joe asked me to talk with her but I wanted to speak with you first," I said.

Our sound screen's volume began changing according to our topic so we quickly discontinued the topic. Sure enough, Sherry jumped in to keep things moving along. She held up a picture of a large-eared character she drew. The picture had an arrow pointing in my direction.

Covering her mouth in laughter, June said, "I'm sorry. That looks very silly."

Sherry stepped over to June's side and touched her hand.

"Schultz said he was gonna talk to the judge," she said.

June picked Sherry up and put her in her lap.

She moved the hair from Sherry's eyes and tucked it behind her ears and asked Sherry to repeat herself.

June faced Sherry but her eyes widened and shifted onto me.

"Silly Man decides if I get to come home or not," Sherry persisted.

I sort of melted out of the lazy boy and crawled over to the small table and chairs. It was time to engage Sherry and let mom slip out the back or at least into the background for a little bit. I reached slowly into the blue scrap paper box and dragged a piece onto the tabletop. But in that short moment, Sherry moved. She went straight over and sat in my lazy boy chair. The bottoms of her shoes were perpendicular to the floor and she placed a sheet of paper on her head.

"Look at me," she announced. "I lost the hair on the very top of my head. I'm Silly Man" she's pointing at me now saying, "You're my patient."

I tried keeping a serious face but when I looked away for just a moment to gain composure, Sherry jumped in front of me.

"Do not laugh at the silly man…."

I couldn't keep my mouth closed and we both burst into a fit of laughter. Kids can truly be teachers, if we're listening close enough. And as I soon found out, she had a lot to teach.

V. All the King's Horses and First Communion

"**D**raw me a picture," Sherry commanded.

"Okay, Mr. Doctor," I acted. "I mean, Mrs. Doctor. I'll draw you a picture."

Sherry stood from the chair and called an audible. "I changed my mind. I want to play with these." She spotted my magnet storybook. These books had theme backgrounds and characters. The theme she selected was called The Magical Castle. Sherry placed the King and Queen magnetic characters outside the castle.

"Which one can I be?" I asked.

From all the choices of people and characters, she refused to give me one. Instead, she chose from the non-people magnets. I got to be a lamppost.

"Oh, come on!" I said. "Give me a person to play."

"There's not enough," she insisted.

"Not enough? There's like seven people characters." I picked up a mean-looking person. "You don't mind if I use this one, right?"

She immediately took it back from me and placed it inside the castle along with a Maid.

"What gives?" I continued to banter.

Sherry proceeded to put a dog and cat near the King and Queen. She had started to unveil her own tailored story. Sherry selected a princess, held it close to my face, and then rotated it back and forth.

"I'm the princess. Here's where I live." She placed the character next to the King and Queen. We have all the strong horses, that helps get food and build stuff."

"Very nice" I commented "I notice you're outside of the castle. What's gonna happen if it rains? Where's your house?"

She was ignoring my questions because it had no place in her narration script.

"Here's what happened," she started. "These two are Tim and Rich."

"Who's who? ...this one is Tim?" I asked.

Clearly not taking questions from the cast at this point, she continued to assign names with characters.

"And this whole area belongs to Mommy and Daddy." She had been sitting 'Indian-style' but now sat up on her knees. I reached for the lamppost that I rejected moments ago.

"When can I shine some light on things?" I smirked.

"Shine it …" she took back the lamp post and demonstrated "like this, right here when I was living at home."

"I'll keep it shining right there," I assured her.

"Not the whole time, only right now," she explained. "The weather'll change, too. You'll see."

Sherry put a sun above her home and then placed the same mean-looking guy that I chose earlier inside the castle.

I assumed a Columbo perspective, "and may I ask why the mean-looking guy is getting the mansion?"

"That's Schultz and…" she randomly grabbed another magnet "this one is Diane."

She was too busy thinking about bringing life to the story board. I couldn't help thinking about how significant June's approval was in getting her to open up. Sherry had learned not to talk about her past life. If she mentioned the longing for her Mommy, Daddy, brothers, grandparents, or even her pets, she believed her mother would go to jail.

Suddenly, there was another change in play. Joe apparently decided he did not want June at the appointment so he arrived unexpectedly at the office to pick Sherry up. The swelling was evident but she tried to hide it. She could hear the two of them arguing down the hall. I managed to hear the words "my First Communion" but she wouldn't elaborate when I asked. One big sniffle followed by a nudge to my arm signaled the 'all clear'.

I looked up to find her sticking her tongue out at me. I thrust my lower jaw out and gave my best hill-billy voice. "Ya'll git sum stuff ta kuv er dat up, 'forez too late. 'Stand I'm tell'n yew?"

She chuckled, wiped her nose and then put her face back down on the table. She was very upset about her mother missing her First Communion. She explained how Schultz misled June to believe the ceremony was a day later. After missing it, she said Schultz began to announce the absence to relatives and teachers, referring to June as uncaring and forgetful.

Gripping a pencil in her fist, she said, "I hate him. I hate him. He told Diane in the car that he told my mom it was on Sunday instead of Saturday." She lifted her head to look at me through red puffy eyes. "How can he hate her so much?"

She put her head back down against the table top, flicking her finger at the corner edge of a piece of paper.

"Man, that's brave," I reached into the rectangular bin of colored pencils. Too much direct talk may shut her down. "Sherry?"

She let loose a moan of stress as her head began to separate from the table surface.

"What?"

"I'm proud of you. That's a big deal for you. It's like you somehow know when it's safe to speak up or something. Were you scared to say something or not really?" I looked down at the scratch paper and doodled for a moment.

"Not really," she said.

"What do you think about me talking to him a little bit? You know, just explain how important it is to you." I said.

"He's not gonna do it. He hates her."

I talked for a short while longer before going to get Schultz.

Entering the lobby, I said, "Hey, Joe. Where's June?" I asked.

"She had to go," he said. That ranks high on the under reporting scale.

"Well, let me meet with you for just a few minutes while Sherry has a seat out here." I waved him back, "Come on back."

Before doing so, however, Joe felt compelled to offer a Public Service Announcement. He opened the door to our dorm-size refrigerator under the sink and pointed at the empty shelves.

"...think you could get a few waters to put in here? This thing is empty every time I've been in here," Schultz said.

I chose to say nothing. He swung the door shut then briefly approached Sherry.

"Here's some goldfish and your book bag. I'll be right out."

As he walks past me, I had a peripheral view of her mocking him. I closed the door to my office and started in on a couple of questions to confirm Sherry's report. Initially, I thought he wouldn't confide in me but I was mistaken.

"Naw, she had the right date, the right time…. The fact is, Sherry's First Communion wasn't on June's priority list." He continued, "You've met her now," he scolded. "She's literally strung out. She can't keep track of dates. This was important to Sherry but apparently, she can't seem to see that."

I had a confused look on my face. "Joe, I'm concerned. She worries about her mother's safety and here, today, she really seems to be interpreting that you didn't want her mom to be there." Pausing a moment, "I mean, she really believes that you're doing stuff deliberately to keep her mom away."

I couldn't leave tonight without knowing whether he understood so I decided to cheat. I gave him an example of a parent's response that fell within normal limits.

"And, Joe, that's not healthy for Sherry's bond with you. It's definitely something that's worth clarifying with her." There, I set it up nicely for him. Just reach out and agree with me. Maybe his response would help me assess his sense of compassion. But I added the evidence statement, "She did say that she had heard you tell Diane that the ceremony was on the following day."

Schultz just stared at me with the same slight smile. I kept up friendly prompts thinking to myself, *Throw me a bone.*

"You remember any kind of talk where she might have heard something that was even close to sounding like that?"

Schultz added a chill to the air when he pulled car keys from his front pocket. "Do you actually think I'd tell her?" He ran the back of his hand across his nose. "She'd just start chaos and screw the entire thing up."

These are continuing signs of brain bruising or whatever kind of neuro-psychiatric thing you want to call it. Like Mark said, he's just not right. Cars have oil filters and humans have social filters. Schultz's filter hasn't been replaced once. His filters are clogged and cause him to perform unreliably. So explaining rudimentary values and

31

relationships with Schultz is moot. His soul is occupied, tethered to a vicious owner, and I don't mean his attorney; although he did manage better when Darla had a script prepared for him. Stepping into my office to answer a few questions, however, was not something Darla would advise this man to do. She's aware of how Schultz's deficits could cause problems for her case. Darla's an evil lady.

He was quick to move toward the door but I had another piece of information.

"One more thing: I received another message from Skip Gilland. He's talking about some tapes that he wanted to send me."

His response was quick "I'll have Darla contact you. She needs to know about any contact with Gilland."

"Okay, that's fine," I said.

Schultz had his cell out of his pocket looking for speed-dial.

"Let me try her office right now."

Oh, boy, this was always a big deal. "This is Joe Schultz. Is Darla in the office?" His eyes rolled up at my office ceiling. "I'm on hold," he said.

I took the opportunity to ask him what he wanted me to do about the message. "Do you have any problem with me contacting him or June?"

"I don't know. Sometimes, she tells me I should've said something then the next time I shouldn't have. So, it's best she tells you. I'm just following her lead."

Joe left the message with Darla's secretary but later the same day Darla called me back and we spoke about her therapy rules.

VI. His Attorney

"This is Danny," I answered.

"Mr. Dawson, Darla Tenor here. How're you this afternoon?" she asked.

"Doing well, thanks."

"Do you have a couple minutes or would it be better to schedule because I can do something mid morning tomorrow if that's better for you. I actually didn't expect you to pick up," Darla said.

"No, no. This is as good as any…. Listen, is there any problem with me contacting this gentleman?" I asked.

She laughed, "Did you say gentleman, Mr. Dawson?"

"Skip Gilland?" I clarified.

"Do you know Skip Gilland had plenty of run-ins with the law, including matters related to his drug addiction?" she continued. "Are you aware that he was committed to a state psychiatric hospital where he received psychiatric treatment?" she disclosed.

"Just the information that Joe told me in our first session but …"

"This guy has a domestic violence charge, possession of a fire arm, the list is scary. I'm tell'n you, he's no gentleman. And you're eager to answer his phone message?" she asked.

"I'm used to a fair amount of collateral contacts working with kids, Ms. Tenor."

"Please, Darla's fine. Call me Darla."

"Okay."

She continues, "What's in the message anyway?"

Why is she so interested in this tape? I'm sure you do this, too, but I tend to have a mental Dewey decimal system where I put information that may come across as perplexing. I really just wanted to get in touch with this guy because of how attached Sherry seems to be with him.

"I don't know anything more than that really. It sounds like he's quite an important person to her," I announced.

"To whom?" Darla asked.

"To Sherry," I said.

"What makes you say that? Is she talking about him?" she asked.

Again, more to file in the card catalog upstairs. She's an attorney. I'm sure she understands all about confidentiality. We would now advance a bit further, cautious of causing too much tilt in neutrality. I say this because Sherry is in her client's residence for the majority of time.

"Would that be a bad thing?" I asked. "She is under the impression that she can't even do that."

"Do what?" she played.

"Simply talk about Mr. Gilland."

"I'll tell you that there is a standing court order that includes specifics about him not having any contact with Sherry." Her volume drops significantly before adding, "And for that matter with June, too."

"Did you say, contact with June?" I asked. "I thought they were only going through a separation right now."

"It's been court ordered that she have no direct or indirect contact with Skip Gilland," she clarified.

I was baffled. "That's really strange," I began. "How did this happen?"

Ms. Tenor was eating something now and I must have caught her in mid bite.

"Like I said, it's in a court order. Listen, I'll have my secretary run a copy for you. I can put that in the mail or even have someone run it over to you today if you'd like."

I felt like I was standing outside, looking in. This would be one of many, many reality checks for me. Ms. Tenor wasn't going to get specific with her answer.

"What I need to know from the court is whether or not Sherry is prohibited from talking about Mr. Gilland. It sounds nuts to me, I don't know that I've ever heard of something like that. I've had cases where the dad murdered the mom and arrangements were made for the kids to visit the guy in prison. Isn't someone talking about basic attachment needs?" I asked.

"Mr. Dawson, there's definitely no misunderstanding," she said "And quite frankly, we're under the belief that June continues to facilitate contact between Gilland and Sherry. Judge Klein was adamant that there be no contact. We all know there has been contact and that June shares matters regarding Sherry with him. You know, we don't want to keep hauling her into court over this. We just want it to end. Gilland is a huge problem and has caused so much irreversible damage. What's your thought on how to end the contact with Gilland?"

I could hear ruffling of what sounded like her lunch bag.

She added, "And, what exactly are you talking about as far as 'attachment needs'? Are you talking about with Mr. Gilland, she has attachment needs?"

I kept in mind the specifics of my release but still I didn't feel comfortable going into these details without the same authorization from June and Sherry.

"Ms. Tenor, I apologize. Let's go ahead and schedule a time where we'll have adequate time." I paused because she laughed.

"Is everything okay?" I confronted.

There was an unusually long silence before she responded.

"Everything's fine," she said.

I continued on with no further regard to her inappropriate slap in my face. I was interested in finding out a bit more about her ethical stance on Sherry. If nothing else, I wanted her to know where I stood.

"The other good thing about us scheduling later is I can get a hold of June in the meantime and run it past her. I think it's a good idea to have both parents' consent whenever possible when it comes to releasing information like we're starting to get into here," I said.

"Mr. Dawson, here's the thing: Have you had any experience with the courts by the way?" she shoved.

"I have, yes. Actually, last week I was flown to Richmond for testimony," I said.

Here's another opportunity to share my position by simply talking experiences where the system works well.

"It was a slick experience. These situations that can be traumatic for people; it's nice to see when players work on behalf of the entire family's best interest."

"How's that? What are you used to working with in domestic court?" She sounded challenging.

35

"In this particular case, the Guardian ad Litem picked me up at the airport, we went straight to the court house and he spent about half an hour asking me about psychosocial history and then what my recommendations relative to custody were. Nothing like these Hoffmann County experiences I'm having. The lengthiest part of the whole thing was the attorneys fighting back and forth about letting me give the testimony. Once I was able to say something about what was causing the child's symptoms in the living environment, things picked up and decisions were made. These cases around here go on forever and, if I'm not mistaken, that's contrary to the AOC's intent for the Family Court. Am I right?"

She was really ignoring a ton of what I was saying at this point.

"So, what kind of decisions are you formulating about Sherry already?"

"Ms. Tenor, can we set aside a time, please," I asked.

"If you'd like to take time to look over your notes so you can be more precise, I'd appreciate it," she jabbed hard that time.

I gave a heavy sigh, "that's what I'll do, Ms. Tenor".

"Don't forget to take a look at the orders, too. You'll find everything you need to follow in those papers. We've come a long way on this case. We didn't want to change therapists because it's more disruptive to Sherry. So, please do a thorough review because we don't want any more interferences. Judge Klein has made that crystal clear, believe me," she said.

What a nice pat on the back that was. She could have just said, "Don't screw with us, little boy." I was more interested in getting off the phone with her even though I was more interested in those previous treatment records.

"I'll definitely take a look at the most recent order," I obliged. "Maybe you could talk with Mr. Schultz about those previous therapy records. I'm not getting anywhere with my requests for those."

"Really, that's the only one you need to be concerned with. I don't expect you to spend your time going over the stuff from years past," she said.

How long were we going to be posturing before she realizes that I'm not her employee?

"You mean the court order?" I asked.

"Right," she said.

"Yeah, I'm talking about treatment records. I need him to sign a release and then I can send away for the..."

"There's nothing different in any other treatment records," she said.

"Ms. Tenor..."

"Darla, you don't have to be so formal, Dan" she reminded.

"Okay. By the way, I actually prefer Danny," I corrected her.

"Sure, I'm sorry 'bout that," she said.

"Communication with previous providers or getting records is like a standard operating procedure. It would be great to especially get a look at the DSS report because I don't know what it was about and I don't know if there are any specific objectives that they would like included," I explained.

"Joe has primary custody so if anything's going to be released by anyone, he's the only person that..."

"I thought it was joint and he has primary physical custody. Is that not correct?"

There was a brief silence.

"Again, I don't think there's anything in any previous records that would be of interest to you but I'll tell you what, I'm gonna go ahead and send you over to Sara." She cut me off.

Just like that, she cut me off. Darla was telling me quite a lot by which questions she was ignoring.

"Sarah?" I asked.

"Yeah, just a sec," she concluded.

Ms. Tenor 'signed off' and I was relayed to her secretary for scheduling.

VII. Mommy Opens Up

I was particularly motivated for today's meeting with June after such a bizarre phone conversation with Tenor. I knew there were missing pieces to the history that Schultz was providing – I just didn't know how much.

We had just sat down; June seemed just a little nervous but she spoke clear and uninhibited.

"So, did you say that you were going to talk with Darla Tenor?" she asked.

"I sure did," I answered.

June let out a long sigh, folded her hands before saying, "I'm surprised you still want to meet with me."

"She's made one thing clear – she does not want "Daddy" in the picture. I'm still puzzled about that," I said.

Her friendly manner accelerated into a more stiff defensive posture.

"I bet there's a lot Joe Schultz and his wife left out when you met with them," she said.

I reached for my paper and pencil.

"I bet you're going to help me out with that, right?" I smiled.

June's hands had a slight tremor that wasn't noticeable until now.

I noticed the slight shaking but shifted eye contact to my paper to give her a moment. She was tentative, trying to hold back tears.

June gave a smile as if to say, "I don't want to cry. I really don't want to cry."

"June, you're feeling somethin' right now. What are you thinking?"

Her lips quivered and tightened. She turned her head side to side. No speech. I waited another moment, surveying peripherally for the Kleenex box. The levy broke immediately.

"I don't know how it got so out of control," her volume was much louder with the sudden sobbing. I put down my pen and paper and stretched across the floor for the Kleenex.

She continued, "They took her," she paused to dab her face. "They took her away." The crying exploded and her breaths broke.

I asked her very slowly, "Take a slow breath with me."

She did. A few deep natural cleansing breaths and she was ready again.

"I'm sorry. I told myself to keep it together but it happened anyway," she said.

Outlining her from head to toe, I said, "...and take a look – you're definitely still all together. Crying is great powerful stuff. I've not seen one person fall apart from it yet."

June smiled, "I see why Sherry likes you so much."

"That's the greatest – I'm so glad to hear she likes our visits," I said.

June gathered up some balls of Kleenex, "Where's your garbage?" she asked.

I stood up to get it from under my desk and asked, "When did things start to get out of control?"

"The minute I opened my big mouth," she snapped.

"What?" I asked.

"Whether you believe me or not, I really did think Skip was her real Dad," her eyes were now wide and alert with energy fueled from her soul.

"He and I, Skip that is, did have some problems but we were working through them. You know, most of our fights were solved eventually. If they gave us a chance, we'd still be together."

I couldn't let her get too far ahead of me.

"Who's they?" I asked.

June looked like I just woke her up.

"What?" she asked.

"I think you said if they gave you a chance...."

"Oh. Yeah, yeah. The whole bunch of them. All of them in the court. As far as I'm concerned, they're all against me. Judge Klein, Tenor, that social worker at Deer County – they forced me to sign my rights away." She stopped to gather herself and then said, "They told me I either sign custody over or I would never see Sherry again."

I was astonished but the look on my face made June uncomfortable.

"You think I'm paranoid?" she asked. "Everyone else is against me and doesn't believe me so I can take it."

"No, June. It's just going at a blur – a fast pace. I want to get this right," I said.

"I'm not sure anyone has an interest in getting it right."

I needed to put the pen and paper down and concentrate on building trust.

I tapped the face of my watch, "I've got plenty of time. If you're willing, then I'm willing."

She was wiping her nose but then froze with my last comment. Kleenex still held to her face, she looked at me for the first time. I recognized the same greeting with victims of abuse who trusted no one.

"I'm not sure where to begin," now looking through a mist of hope.

"You're doing just fine telling me about players involved. Go ahead and tell me again about Deer County and the social worker. Maybe how the DSS case got from Deer to Hoffmann."

"You seriously have enough time to go through this?"

"Yup," I answered.

"I'll need to go way back because you should hear it from the beginning," she said.

"There was more than just the one person that day at Deer County. There were several people in that room when they forced me to sign those papers – but I'll explain that...." She repositioned herself sitting back on the sofa.

"Okay. Sure, that's fine," I said.

"Well, I started to say that it all happened because I opened my big mouth – what I meant is when I told Joe Schultz that I thought Sherry was his child," she said.

"But, you thought Joe Gilland was her real Dad. Isn't that what you were saying?" I clarified.

"Yeah, but I mean that was when she was smaller. Before I could really..." looking away "...you know, recognize the features."

She looked disappointed suddenly. I stopped taking notes to see what had happened.

"What's happening?" I asked.

"Nothing," she hesitated "I don't really expect anyone to believe me. See, Skip Gilland and I didn't marry until after she was born. We were serious and planned to get married but we had a fight and stayed in separated places for about a month." She looked down near the floor.

"But, obviously, like you said, patched things up well enough to get back together and get married," I furthered.

"Not before I did something." She looked up at me. "I knew Joe Schultz. I stayed at his place and, Sherry came from a night where I allowed myself to get intimate with him."

"Okay," I said. I didn't want her to break her pace. She was falling into the content as if staring at an old photo album.

"I swear to you," with her right hand raised in the air "I didn't think he was the father."

Again, she looked at the floor.

"I sound like I have no clue don't I? You think I'm...."

"June. I am not thinking anything other than paying attention closely to what you're saying right now," I raised my eyebrows "Okay?"

She nodded.

I encouraged her, "Please go on. I'm listening."

"I don't know. I really don't know where to go from here, there's so much," she said.

"Where did Joe Schultz exit and Skip Gilland come back," I asked.

"Oh, we were back together within the next couple of weeks. I guess my ignorant thinking that since every other time was with Gilland, that one time with Schultz didn't even enter my mind." Shaking her head, she added "Until a little later."

"So, the entire pregnancy, Joe Gilland was with you?" I asked.

"Yeah...except he was not happy about the idea of being a father. He didn't know if we were ready for marriage so he didn't think it was right to bring a child into the world," she said.

"So, you stayed firm and determined?"

41

"Yeah. There was no way anything else would happen but to have the baby. Even if adoption was the answer. I wasn't having an abortion. I don't know how to explain it," she said.

"Your're explaining it fine," I assured her again.

Her voice picked up, "Here's the real amazing thing," she started.

"Skip Gilland didn't like the idea one bit, I mean not at all. I was really worried when Sherry was born and felt like I'd be living my life as a single parent raising her and my sons without Gilland. But if you saw Gilland's face the first time he saw her, you'd see a man transforming in front of your eyes," she said.

"Really?"

"Really. I am not exaggerating at all; once he picked her up that first time, it was next to impossible to separate them," her smile was broad, her eyes filling with joy.

"Wow." I said "That's beautiful, June."

Beautiful and really chilling – who in their right mind would interfere with this bond?

"June, was it quite some time before Skip Gilland saw Sherry after her birth or about how long was it until he held her for that first time?"

"Oh, geez, the next day," she replied.

A dreary, cold atmosphere seeped across a macro canvas, there would be no rational explanation for severing this bond. This was the product of a closed system where motives and malice go together like peanut butter and jelly.

"So, Skip Gilland held her the day after she was born?" I confirmed.

She still had that toasty smile on her face as she looked right through me. "Yup," she said. "And, see he stayed with her during the day while I worked full time," she said.

She had my undivided attention.

"Why's that?" I asked.

"Because of his back, he fortunately collects disability because of an on-the-job-accident. It was horrible."

I cringed but tried keeping her on the early attachment history. "He was there with her, literally every day from the second day of her life."

"Or more like every second from the second day of her life."

"Yeah, that's exactly right," she replied.

"And what exactly did Skip Gilland do that got him in so much trouble that he could no longer see her?" I asked.

"I don't know what you mean by 'trouble'," she said.

"Well, what's the reason that his rights were taken away?" I asked.

June stared at me. Stared and stared until I shrugged my shoulders in a confused way.

"What?" I asked.

"Who are you, Danny Dawson?" she asked.

"I'm a social worker. I mostly work with families and kids," I said.

"Well, I know that," she laughed. "I haven't been asked these kinds of questions, even by DSS."

She took a really deep sigh before resuming with a response to my question.

"I know one thing relates to his psychiatric admission," she said.

"What was he admitted for?"

"Having a nightmare, this nightmare unloaded into his reality. As quick as his life changed when she came in, it was just as quick when he was taken out of hers," June began to sob. "Could they put themselves in his shoes? How would you respond if one day your wife came to you begging forgiveness before even telling you, telling you how horribly sorry she was…that before you married she was with someone else. And then you hear that your own daughter…" crying almost uncontrollably again, she manages to finish, "…isn't really your biological daughter?"

June was thumbing through a bag of papers as she was responding to questions.

"I remember right exactly where I was when the thought hit me. She stood near this window," again, June was in a daze as she recalled the moment "and the lighting… I don't know how else to describe seeing her. You know, recognizing features and at the same time thinking about the possibility of Schultz being her biological dad." Her head bowed, "It was too clear, I really knew it from that moment on."

June stopped and handed me a small stack of papers.

I fanned the pages, noting the legal headlines.

"Joe will be giving me a copy but do you have custody rights now?" I asked.

"Yeah. We have joint legal custody, but now he has primary physical custody," she said.

Confirming my intuition, this was contrary to what Schultz had told me.

"Why? What did he say, he had…sole custody or something?" she questioned.

I scooted away from the topic by addressing the top page on the stack.

"No worries, I just want to make sure I've got it right," I passed on any elaboration. "So, the paternity testing was in 2003?" I asked.

"I think so," she replied.

I took time to briefly look over the documents. At the top right of the first page it read:

04SP 2041
HEARSAY DISCLOSURE NOTICE

There's a short paragraph followed by a center page announcement:

Paternity Testing Corporation Joseph Schultz has a 99.999% probability of being the biological father of Sherry June Gilland.

I looked at the disclosure notice. "She has his name?"

"Yup. They seem to have a hard time accepting that," she said calmly.

"There you go saying 'they,'" I highlighted.

"I mean, basically Tenor and Klein," she focused.

"That's his attorney and the judge?" I hesitated. "And you're saying what? That they're somehow biased?" I asked.

"It sure feels like it," she answered. June was again going through various papers. Her emotions were running higher. "By the way," June said, "they fire people that don't do it their way."

I quickly looked up, "What do you mean?" I asked.

She laughed, "It's not looking so good for you, now that I think about it. Since Sherry and I both like you, they'll hate you."

June turned another single document so that it was facing me on the table. "Here's one that might interest you," she said.

The letter is written by a private psychologist:

To Whom It May Concern,

At the request of Sherry Gilland's mother, I am writing this letter for the Court to state that Sherry has been receiving counseling to help provide her with additional support through this time of transition with some family issues (e.g., paternity issues, visitation with biological father).

It is my understanding that Sherry believes Mr. Gilland is her father, and does not think of Mr. Schultz in this regard. She has had several opportunities to discuss people important to her in our sessions, and she has not voluntarily mentioned Mr. Schultz in any of our sessions. When I mention Mr. Schultz's name, she states that she does not want to discuss him. When encouraged to do so, Sherry mentioned that she had spent time with Mr. Schultz and that he had a picture or poster in his bedroom that was frightening to her. She chose not to elaborate much more on this topic when encouraged to do so.

Sherry views her family unit as consisting of her mother, Mr. Gilland (she refers to him as 'Daddy'), and two brothers. It is my understanding that she does not know of the biological relationship that exists between her and Mr. Schultz. Thus, past visitations with Mr. Schultz have been discussed within the context of a family friend relationship.

In determining any possible future visitation with Mr. Schultz, I would strongly recommend that Sherry's emotional status be given much thoughtful consideration. All parties involved, possibly with the assistance of a court-appointed psychologist or clinical social worker, need to carefully consider the impact of how Mr. Schultz's relationship has already impacted Sherry and how any possible future relationship with Sherry should be presented to her. Based on information reported by Sherry, I would have concerns about the impact on Sherry's social and emotional functioning if visitation resumed with Mr. Schultz.

Elizabeth Thomas, Ph.D.

I held the document up. "I guess things changed or something since this was written."

"You can have that, it's a copy," she said. "The one thing that hasn't changed at all is how stuff like this is totally ignored by the court."

The documents kept surfacing as if from a magician's hat.

"Like, look at this one," she handed another to me. "This one is written by my old attorney to Schultz's attorney."

"To Tenor?" I confirmed.

"Yeah, she's been on this pretty much from the very beginning. Schultz somehow never runs out of money but I can't afford it. Plus, it's not doing me any good."

A paragraph in this particular document from her attorney to Schultz's attorney struck my attention:

I have been informed that Deer County DSS and two separate private mental health clinicians would like to schedule a meeting of all adults involved in this case, including Mr. Skip Gilland, in the near future. It seems that the desire is to make sure that all parties understand of DSS's role in this case and to assist everyone in understanding the overall goal(s) of the department. I believe this meeting would be most helpful to the parents. We, as the representing attorneys, will be offered the opportunity to attend the meeting. As there is a remaining question as to why the current temporary order requires that June not be in the presence of Mr. Gilland, the department is willing to have their attorney draft a letter informing the court that the meeting was at their request and not intended to frustrate or violate the order of the court. Please, advise as to whether you require such letter be submitted prior to said meeting.

"Yes!" I celebrated. "See here, this is good stuff."

"Good stuff?" she asked.

"Yeah, look at this. Right here it says that ALL adults need to sit down and get things straight. They think "Daddy" needs to be in the picture, too. We can get everyone together, right?" I asked.

June interrupted, "…unless you want to get yourself fired even faster. They don't mess around, Danny. They don't want Skip in her life, period." Before I could reference the letter again, she said, "Take a look at his attorney's response."

The letter in part states:

At this time we do not agree to having a meeting. Who from DSS recommended that this meeting take place? Please provide me with their names and numbers.

Yikes! What's she going to do, take them for a long ride somewhere?

We have no interest in anything that will include Skip Gilland. Judge Klein has been very clear in her directive that Mr. Gilland not be involved with Sherry. In addition, your client should have no direct or indirect communications with him. We believe any such meeting would be in violation of the order and a letter from Social Services would not excuse such violation.

June could see the message was sinking in with me.

"Now, you see, right?" she asked me.

"What came from this? I mean, how did DSS decide to approach it if the judge opposed having everyone meet together?"

"Like I said, they don't mess around. If someone gets in the way of Klein or Tenor, they get rid of them," she replied.

"So, it just never took place at all?" I asked.

"Nope. But there were more letters exchanged between Tenor and DSS about all of this," she rapidly started going through papers "I'm sure I can get my hands on them if you're interested."

In further readings from copies I made from June's documents, I found psychological evaluations were performed on *"all adults directly involved in Sherry' life."* June told me that the psychologist discussed her results and she didn't recall anything negative that was revealed. She, however, said that the records were somehow "lost" in the court somewhere. The psychological evaluations of June, Skip Gilland, Joe Schultz, and Diane Schultz were completely lost while stored inside the courthouse.

Another interesting matter that came from this appointment with June today was that DSS in Deer County had a pediatric psychologist that interviewed Sherry. This DSS specialist documented grave concern about the relationship Sherry had with her previous therapist. It was this pediatric psychologist that referred Sherry to me. The psychologist identified that Sherry felt strongly that her therapist was "on Schultz's side" and "told mean stories about Daddy." These stories included the acceptance of him sexually molesting her. Eerie setup, if that's what's going on. Tenor apparently recommended this first therapist. How does that work? Something pungent is coming through. This is all seeming a lot bent. There's so much documentation, letters, emails, evaluations, but only a few will be directly referenced. This is one of them because it is one of the few that succinctly emphasizes what the main focus of all of this needs to be on.

The letter was written to Darla Tenor from June's attorney:

I have both listened to your voicemail and reviewed your letter. Obviously, we disagree on the issue regarding replacing her current therapist. I had hoped that I had made it clear that the change is not at the impetus of June. The therapists who have recommended the change were consulted in conjunction with the work an/or investigation being done by Deer County DSS. Dr. Finegold, whose name I may be spelling incorrectly, performed psychological evaluations of all adults. Dr. Shaffer actually met with Sherry at the behest of DSS and likewise is of the opinion that replacing her current therapist would benefit both child and parents. As such, we believe that their recommendation should be followed.

I am of the firm opinion that both parents have to begin yielding their personal wills in order to safe-guard the mental and emotional development of Sherry. This is not about control, it is about making sure Sherry survives the many changes in her life. Therefore, I respectfully request that you you take the time to speak with Ms. Phillips at DSS so that you may obtain contact information for the above named therapist. Perhaps a conversation with them will assist you in understanding the reason(s) for the suggested change.

In regards to the meeting with DSS, I would again defer to the clinical recommendations of the department which was to include Mr. Skip Gilland. The suggestion of DSS seemed to be aimed at allowing all adults who have played a significant role in Sherry's life to hear the department's concerns and goals. If you will consider Mr. Gilland's presence a violation of the order, I will simply recommend to the department that they take such steps as may be necessary to assure the court as to the purpose and nature of the meeting. It was helpful to hear the department's explanation in a recent phone call. I would again suggest that you contact DSS because I will say that as much as it may disturb the parents, it may be difficult to treat and/or help Sherry develop the healthy attitude that is so important to her well being without understanding the confusion she must feel. There is a difference between knowledge and heart felt application of that knowledge. As such, some things come only with time and consistent demonstration of the feelings to be associated with that which is known.

I am sure that we will receive from the department those dates which they suggest for a meeting. Until that time, I am in hopes that we can reach some agreement regarding Sherry's therapist. I will be in the office most of the week. Please feel free to call me if you wish to discuss any of these issues.

Cc: Cindy Riechert / Deer Co Social Services
Tina Draper

Our session concluded eventually, and I sat with my door closed in my office. I was leaning forward, bracing my arms to my knees and gazing out the window. Could all of this be true?

VIII. Spies and Willy Wonka

W alking in from the parking lot, I heard a knocking sound from the lobby window. When I looked up, I saw Mark motioning for me to pick up my cadence.

"Diane called you," he said handing me a message sheet. "She basically just wants you to know that Sherry's telling her about nightmares and wants you to talk with her about them today," he said.

"Alright," I acknowledged.

"Hey, that's not all," Mark held his thumb and pinky simulating a telephone, "June's on the phone. She wants to catch you before you see Sherry this morning."

I took the call in Mark's office. "Good morning, this is Danny."

"Hey, it's June. I'm sorry to be calling so early," she said.

"No apology necessary. Now that I'm talking with you, I remember what this is about...."

"You wanted me to let you know when I spoke with Sherry, right? About Gilland and seeing him."

"That's it, how did the conversation go?"

"Danny, I'm a little nervous that she'll have to start over with another therapist," June said. "Darla Tenor called to tell me that Klein doesn't want me talking to you so much. She thinks I need my own therapist."

What in the world is going on now? The order spells out that I am appointed for individual and family therapy. I wasn't going to get her worked up.

"Let's not do anything she's not ready to do," I interrupted.

"No, no. She's fine with talking about it, but I just think it's gonna be a little on the weird side because she's so used to trouble of some kind when she opens up or if I open up about him," she explained.

The sadness of the situation, a sense of hopelessness in any total disclosure was alarmingly obvious. I was one of how many professionals involved to this point.

"I'll just check it out, get a sense of where's she's at after having talked with you."

51

"I told her it was okay and she seemed fine with it but she knows the language," June said.

"Language?" I asked.

"She'll probably say something about the judge's order. It's where the whole fear of me going to jail comes in," she said.

"I know it doesn't secure much, but I'll reaffirm what Joe has said about it being the goal for Sherry to feel fully comfortable and feel free to talk about anything at all," I said.

Following my conversation with her, I did just that and Joe gave a resounding "Of course."

Sherry's enthusiasm wasn't the same today. She saw my family tree from our initial meeting. It was sitting on the small table.

She did a fly-by the table top, "What're we doin' today?" She seemed agitated with me.

"Mom said she spoke with you about some stuff. She told me she told you it was okay to talk about Daddy and even your Dad …"

She whacked me in the head with a stuffed animal.

"Hey! What was that for?" I asked.

"Don't call him my Dad," she demanded.

I had a look on my face like I lost my car keys.

"Schultz told me you're gonna get me to call him Dad," as she punished a stuffed animal, punting and punching around the office. "Good luck. He's not my Dad if I don't want him to be."

I just waited. Not a big deal. Red lights are even longer.

"You wouldn't trick me," she coached herself. "He's lying again, I know it."

Reticence was serving my position well, I continued to let her do the talking.

"Did you or didn't you tell him that?"

She'll make a great prosecutor some day.

"I did not tell Mr. Schultz that I would get you to call him 'Dad'." I admitted.

Partly embarrassment, partly frustration, she covered her ears and put her head down on the table.

"I want my mommy" she said "I just want to go back home," she was shutting down.

I asked, "Would you like to call her?"

She popped her head back up, "Yeah, can we call her?"

"I don't see why not," I replied.

"Yes!" she exclaimed "Here, let me dial," she said.

Sherry dialed and, as requested, handed the phone back to me when it started ringing.

June answered, "Hey, Danny".

"Hello, June. Guess who I have with me in the office right now?"

June was in her cubicle at work and spoke softly. "So how's everything going over? Is she talking about him?"

"Well, I think it would be great if you'd maybe reinforce that part about disclosure." I thought I might have slid the vocabulary by Sherry but something told me otherwise. I hoped it was worded well enough.

"I see," she acknowledged. "Sure, I'd be glad to. Just so you know, Schultz probably hasn't shared with you, she's crying a whole lot more. Diane's actually been emailing me for help, if you can believe that. He'll put a stop to her doin' that, just wait."

"Fantastic. I'll give her the phone and then she can just hang up afterward. Sorry to be so short but she's ready to talk to you right now."

I handed Sherry the phone.

"Mommy?" she checked.

It was like someone put a warm blanket around her. But Sherry wanted privacy.

"Cover your ears, Silly Man" she instructed.

I looked behind me as if she may have been referring to someone else.

"Mommy, just a minute" she held the phone at her side. "I'm talking to YOU, Danny Fanny," she said, pointing at me with the other hand.

I covered my ears, but didn't plug them. She went under my desk and kept her back to me. I heard Sherry say, "Are you sure?" and "I don't want you to go to jail, Mommy". Then came "Okay. Okay. I will."

She crawled out from under the desk and shouted, "You can hear now!"

I smiled, "Is everything good?"

"My mommy wants me to tell you how I felt about her and Daddy," she said.

I moved closer by scooting my chair a little bit.

"That's great," I replied, "but is that what you want, or no?"

She started pulling on a koosh ball.

"I want him to stop waking me up like he does," she got up and pulled me by the wrist. "Come over here and lay down on the couch like you're me sleeping in bed."

We were obviously still going to talk about frustrations with Schultz. I curled up with a stuffed animal.

"Close your eyes!" she said before turning off my office lights. She stepped outside the door for just a moment. She then barged in as if it were Christmas morning. The lights came on and her voice was a piercing demand.

"Get up!" she changed her tone back for a second to say "Pretend you have covers on."

She yanks the covers off and walks out of my office leaving the door wide open. Since Mommy's 'green light', there was definitely less inhibition about sensitive topics. The other therapists had their doors closed but the stomping was almost too much. I stayed put, even though it was hard having her out of my sight for a few moments. I didn't chase her. I kept thinking, *There's nothing for her to get into in the hallway. She'll be back.* And sure enough, the stomping crescendo brought her back. She entered my office but left the door wide open. She then randomly started pounding on my lazy boy chair as if playing a set of bongos.

"That's how my heart goes when I wake up," she said.

One of my colleagues came out and gave me a look of "Everything okay?"

I waved and then quietly closed the door.

"I'm sorry that happens, Sherry," I said.

She walked over to my desk and picked up my phone.

"Hello, Judge Klein? Are you the one that took my Mommy and Daddy? Are you the one that sent the spies?" she acted.

I tried to get a word in before the topic changed again.

"Spies? What are…?"

"I want to go home!" she yelled into the receiver before slamming it down. "I want those spies to stop bothering me and my mom. They're everywhere," she said.

"Spies?" I asked.

"Spies. Yes, spies." With a colored pencil, she began to draw on the scratch paper. "The truck is dark blue and it goes wherever we go." She was flushed from the physical exertion. "That's how he found out when Mommy brought me here that one time."

My mind flashed back to that day and it did seem very odd that he managed to pin down the exact day and time of her appointment.

In the picture she was drawing, the driver appeared to be a man with a baseball hat and beard. He was an angry-looking guy. Sherry tapped the pencil on the driver's face "This is the spy guy," she announced.

All I could do was sit still. I could hear my internship supervisor in the back of my head coaching, "Know when to say nothing". It just seemed lately I was doing a lot of that with kids.

Sherry started drawing a wavy line across the paper. "This one time, we went from mommy's house," she said, dragging her pencil backwards to the start of the line, "all the way to my school and then to Daddy's mommy and Daddy's house."

A sudden sneeze resulted in a cannon of goo all over her canvas. This had a very low stress impact compared to what she was dealing with on a daily basis. She sniffed big and gave the back of her hand a clear sheath.

"Ouch," I said reaching for the Kleenex box.

"Oh, well," she crumpled the paper "I can draw it better anyway."

After setting the stage on paper once again, she continued, "But the spies followed right on the back of our car," she pointed with her finger at the space between her mom's car and the blue truck, "right where my fingernail is," she said.

Sherry was building up her breathing, the rate was definitely increasing.

"I'm listening," I said softly and slowly "but look at my nose for a sec."

Sherry stopped to look at me. I placed my palms face down on the table.

"Will you put your hands on top of mine?" The pencil dropped from her hand and we both watched it roll through molasses before dropping to the floor.

"Take one or two deep, and really, really slow, slow breaths with me, okay?"

I made my voice sound like my battery was wearing down. I pointed at my nose.

"Nose," I paused "then out through your mouth."

As she exhaled on her first attempt, she ended quickly so she could talk sooner.

"Danny?" she asked

"Yup?" I answered

"Thank you for doing this for me," she said.

I was amazed.

"You mean talking with you?" I asked.

"Just help'n me be happy. You know?" she said. Her eyes filled quickly and a heavy stream ran down her face.

"But those look like tears. What are you thinking right now, Sherry?" I asked.

She shook her head as if to say 'forget it.'

"Please? This is important, I really want to know what you're thinking," I repeated.

She laid her head down on the table. "He's gonna fire you," she said.

"What? You mean...." I pointed to the lobby.

She nodded "I heard him talking with Diane two nights ago," she stood and walked away from the little table and chairs. She picked up another stuffed animal but this time it was for curling up with and cuddling.

"Umm...," speechless yet again. "Maybe not," I reached.

"That lady he talks to about Mommy wants him to get everything you've written down about me and then find someone else for me to start talking to," she said.

"I think I know who you're talking about," I said.

"Darla, that's who," she said "She's the one that Schultz told about Daddy touching my private area".

If I was on video tape, I'm sure I looked like a deer in headlights.

"Do you want to tell me about that a little?" I asked.

"I don't know," she paused, "but Daddy would never do that. Why don't they ever think Schultz does anything wrong? He's the reason my pee pee was hurting anyway. He never got in trouble for that," she said.

"You told the other therapist that he was the reason your pee pee was hurting?" I confirmed.

"Yeah. I said what I told everyone; I told her the same thing," she said.

"What's that? What did you tell everyone?"

"The true story. That I know he put his finger in my private part so far it hurt my tummy," she again fled with the stuffed animal, but this time hid her face in the oversized office chair. "He grosses me out!" she made a face that looked like she just took some cough medicine "He's always walking around in his underwear and I can see his 'willy wonka'," she said. I spent some time with drawing and, from what she communicated, he was not exposing his penis but frequently interacted with her with only his underwear on.

"So, how did that name willy wonka come up?" I asked.

"Schultz calls it his willy wonka," she answered.

There was a knock at my office door. I glanced at my watch and noticed that I had gone ten minutes over.

I opened the door to find Mark. "He's wants to bring her shopping so...."

"Tell him I need time with him. If not right now, then later tonight. Tomorrow's too late in other words."

Mark looked at me like I was forgetting something, "You've got a 6:00 tonight."

"Then you can offer 7:00 P.M. I need to see him tonight." I wasn't finished either. "And tell him I need fifteen more minutes." That was daring.

As soon as the door closed, Sherry continued "I just want to talk with Judge Klein."

"I'll find out if you can do that," I said.

"Mommy thinks you're nice," she said.

"That's really great. I think your mommy is a nice person, too."

"She won't go to jail just because I'm tell'n you stuff. She told me that."

"That's why you haven't wanted to talk with me about all these things?" I asked.

"I did talk all about this same stuff before and that really fat lady" she looked at me confused. "You know, she's like you. She's a talking doctor," she continued, "except she didn't listen to me. She just wanted me to call him 'Dad' and then Schultz told me 'It's none of anyone's business,'" Sherry said.

"You mean about him wearing underwear around you?"

"Yeah," she answered "I want my old bed back so I can sleep."

"Diane wanted me to talk with you about your nightmares. I forgot to bring that up today."

"Those are scary." She put her hands up to her face. "Those are about the car!" she gasped.

"Here," I gently slid paper across the table for her to draw but she wanted to act instead.

"This is the front of the car where the steering wheel is okay?" she leaned forward and put her hand under the seat. "Right here, Schultz has some rope and a knife."

"Under his seat in the car? You've seen it?" I clarified.

"He won't tell me what he's doin' with it," she said.

My office door suddenly flew open and I experienced the bongo beating first hand.

"We gotta go. Now." Schultz stood with a hand on his hip.

I casually gathered the drawings and placed them on my desk. Sherry began collecting her own materials while I positioned myself quite close to Schultz.

"We need to meet," I said.

"Why?" he asked.

I used the only language that would lasso him into compliance, "Let me just say this is something Darla will need to be aware of ASAP."

As if it was something substantial for the upcoming hearing, he replied "Sure, sure. Today?"

"I'll stay late this evening – how about 7:00? Can you be here?" I asked.

"I'll be here," he replied.

IX. You're Fired

"Thanks so much for taking time to meet."
I reached across with two copies of a treatment summary. They looked like a couple of K9s getting their first drink of water after a day in the sun.

"You made this meeting sound like it was an emergency or something," he slurped.

I noticed Diane give a supportive chuckle as she read over the first page. I hadn't seen that from her before – she had her game face on I guess. I placed my original on a side table.

"It is fairly urgent, Joe." I waited but he wouldn't look up.

Diane elbowed Joe after spending a few seconds on the second page. She pointed at the page, and whispered, "Look at number three on page two."

Joe turned the page over abruptly. I was silent.

"What do you call this? An assessment?" He had a growling twitch but no teeth showing yet. Without my immediate response, he continued his threatening tone. "You contracted to verify June's compliance with her own psychiatrist. Have you done that yet?"

I maintained eye contact and relaxed my face. There is no such 'contract'. I couldn't help thinking that he and Darla didn't want me talking to other providers. He wasn't too good with non-verbals but the look was one of disappointment. I just waited to see what tone might follow this but he let it drip away from the rest of our talk.

"What's this about?" he said, referring to the recommendations on the second page.

"Which one are you looking at?" I asked.

"Any one of them," Diane was now clearly a bold supporter of Joe at this point.

"Yeah. What are we supposed to do with this?" Joe demanded.

At this moment it was no longer a "maybe' about this being my last meeting. He probably was encouraged to attend by his attorney but I think this would be it.

In an effort to neutralize the air I said, "Let me read over that second page and we'll discuss each one if you'd like." I paused. "I'm obligated to follow up with DSS given Sherry's report about a few things earlier today. It may or may not relate the previous report, but I'll let them do what they need to do with the information."

"DSS?" he asked.

I provided him with just enough details about what Sherry disclosed at the session earlier in the day. Neither Joe nor Diane expressed concern about it. No clarification or questions asked.

Joe wasn't feeling in control so he took it where ever he could.

"This one: Sherry has expressed a strong sense of loss from Skip Gilland and his family'. How about getting to the point? Are you saying, go against Judge Klein's court order?" he slammed.

The probability of Joe being a perpetrator grew twenty-fold after ignoring the information that I just gave to him. I had really done some decent maturing over the past couple decades. As a kid, this is right about when I'd step into the breath of a bully to ask that he put the ball in play. Something like, 'Hit me so we can exercise together." Not an ego deficit but a duty to act.

Joe kept his avoidance of eye contact and kept hurling sticks and stones.

"You're a child therapist?" he patronized. Both he and Diane had a good chuckle. "And your answer to everything is to… let me get this straight, break a court order and put my daughter in the hands of a dangerous felon?"

Still no eye contact but his face was beet red.

"What do you want to see happen. I mean what happens if she seeks him out in later years?"

"We can leave the country. I'd leave the country if we had to," he answered swiftly.

"On the first page, you'll see that I give some support to how early school age development applies but in bold you see "Keep in mind the quality of her attachment with you". What I mean by that is her perception of you can be based on whether she feels that you prevent her from leaving other secure people attachment figures in her life," I explained.

61

"There's no way," he flipped his copy onto Diane's lap.

I decided to play a card that I don't typically but figured using his language helped keep conversation pointed.

"The court order has a couple things that might need some clarifying then," I said.

"Like what," he snapped.

"The discretion given to me in deciding to work with family members together in session with Sherry."

"There isn't anything that says that in the court order," he said.

A thrust of energy came over me; now was the moment.

"See, this may be where our communication is breaking up. There's some discrepancies in the reports I'm being given," I started.

"Please, go on" Schultz interjected as he repositioned back into the sofa.

A flash of lightning and crackling thunder will follow Schultz's statement, if ever a theatrical version is made.

"Go on?" I covered my head as if an anvil was about to fall.

With a threatening squint, Schultz replied, "Sure. This'll be good. Darla wants to hear this, too."

Maybe Ms. Tenor isn't as bad as he makes her out to be but I continued to associate Darla Tenor with Darth Vader or the Godfather. A really creepy mix of big brother and anything else you can think of that's evil.

"I wanted to get clear about recommendations of previous providers and that initial DSS report." I took a breath quickly to discourage any territorial take-over "...cause as it turns out, they're apparently similar to the ones I'm giving to you right now."

Joe stood up and motioned for Diane to follow behind him. Something about people reading previous records struck a bad chord.

"I guess that would also mean you were doing that without my written consent?" he said.

"Joe, I received the information from..."

He pointed at me, "YOU'RE FIRED! Hear me, okay? Fired."

He led Diane toward the door.

Maybe there was time for one more sentence, "I thought I was appointed by the court?"

He kept walking. I kept trying.

"Wait!" I stood to follow behind as they walked down the hallway "She needs to continue her treatment, Joe. She's just beginning to open up with me. This is too abrupt. Remember the talks we've had about symptoms of anxiety and depression? I want you to have her see a psychiatrist," I said.

He turned around in a fury. "You know why she has anxiety? Because you're probably tell'n her she can see June and Skip. Anybody would be anxious if they had to think about see'n a criminal. Don't worry, I'll find her someone new. That's not your concern anymore."

"Then, please, contact me as soon as possible with the new provider's name so I can document it, Joe."

The weight of my head fell back and I stared at the ceiling before walking back into my office. For the child, this is where the front line emerged. They're left alone to deal with the after-shocks of their disclosures. I needed to know that DSS was going to take the case and hear what concerns remained for Sherry's safety. Laws pertaining to confidentiality somehow prohibited DSS from providing information about the initial report. Subsequently, they're getting the case back with minimal progress.

Schultz promulgated the news rather quickly because phone messages surfaced the very next morning.

"Call for you on line two," Mark said "It's Darla Tenor."

I didn't have to take the call but I also didn't want any surprises later on.

"This is Danny."

"Mr. Dawson. I understand my client fired you last night," she said.

"He mentioned that, yes" I responded, "but I'm not sure he can do that given my name is assigned in the order. The quandary I'm having is how to get Sherry the treatment she's needing right now because…"

"Mr. Dawson, we're under the belief at this point that you're supporting Sherry's mother" she interrupted.

"I'm supporting the idea of family." I paused before emphasizing, "but I'm employed by Sherry. According to state statutes, that is."

63

I didn't have the statute code in front of me at the time so it was convenient that she moved on.

"I requested notes from your phone conversations with Gilland. Do you remember that?" she asked.

Suddenly I felt as if I was being recorded.

"I remember your interest in the tapes he spoke about," I replied.

"Go ahead and tell me what's on those tapes. By now I'd assume you've listened to them."

"Nope. I never received any tapes." I said.

"Mr. Dawson, someone's not being completely honest here. Mr. Schultz informs me that you've looked at some information about Sherry's previous treatment, is that not accurate?"

"I did and…"

Again, she cut me off

"Listen, here's what I'm primarily interested in – are you going to testify in support of June getting custody?" she stopped herself "Let me rephrase that. Are you in agreement that Ms. Gilland is unfit based on her refusing to follow the court order and putting Sherry in harm's way?"

"And 'harms way' would mean facilitating contact with Mr. Gilland?" I asked.

"Correct," Darla answered.

Without hesitation, "Then, absolutely, I am not in agreement with that statement."

In her own special way, Darla declared war.

"Okay, here's what I need from you then," she instructed, "since the hearing is less than a month away, I'll need a copy of your chart."

"A copy of Sherry's chart?

"Yeah, then you won't need to be bothered with wondering whether we'll be calling you to testify on this or that," Darla led.

I was curious about who tolerated her leash training in the past in order for her to deliver with such conviction.

"Uh, oh" I started.

"What's the matter?" she asked.

"A case summary is something I can do but are you talking about psychotherapy notes?" I knew that was exactly what she meant.

There was a sigh followed by a teeth grit chuckle. "Whatever you have on this case, yes, Mr. Dawson."

She's addressing me as Mr. Dawson? Where was the tightness we once had?

"I can't do that, Darla," I said. "I'm sure you're familiar with HIPAA laws.

"Oh, quite familiar, Mr. Dawson" I felt like she had the neck of my shirt in her fist. "I figured you also were aware of the rights Mr. Schultz has in requesting those records given the fact that he has primary."

That was a mean thing for her to do. She was trying to bully me into believing he had sole custody again.

"You'll have to give me some guidance here." I played. "I thought they had a joint arrangement with Joe having primary residence beginning a year ago or something like that."

She quickly recalibrated.

"Either way," another deep sigh "I can subpoena the notes or make a phone call to Klein and have an order sent certified this afternoon."

And that would be a body slam and point of tap out for me. No consideration of Sherry's rights whatsoever.

"I guess I'll wait for the order then."

"Real sorry things worked out like this," she may have been examining last week's manicure.

"It sure is a rude awakening, I'll say that," I moaned.

"Is there something in particular you don't want us to see in the record?" she
asked.

"I need to get going, if you don't mind." I must have sounded sick. I sure felt like it.

"Sure, sure. I'll go ahead and have Judge Klein put that together tomorrow and then, like I say, it won't be necessary for you to be at the hearing."

X. There's Blood

Liability had a throbbing pulse. If Darla could influence Klein that easily, then protecting Sherry's rights was going to be difficult. How could I know if Sherry was receiving treatment if Schultz prevented me from having communication with anyone?

5/23/xxxx 2:07:52PM

Voicemail message left for me from June:

"Danny, it's June. I just got an email from Joe saying he had to let you go. So, Sherry was right. He keeps taking good people away from her. I just still can't believe he can keep doing shit like this without talking to me. Excuse my language, I'm sorry. Let me tell you something, Sherry's a mess with him so mad. He and Darla were counting on your testimony so they had something to keep my visitation in limbo. He said working with you has been a complete waste of time and money. I was really looking forward to our meeting on the seventh with Sherry. Are you still going to meet with me? If you'd please let me know, I really hope so. I'm telling you something's worse over there. Call me when you get this because Sherry's tell'n me they finally took her to Dr. Lawrence and there's blood in her urine. Call me, Danny. I'll wait to hear back. Thanks, Bye."

I was copying Sherry's records, standing five feet away from the speaker. Schultz never gave me consent to speak with her pediatrician but I'd take that risk in order to confirm what I just heard. Dr. Lawrence and I worked together at the HMO. I'm positive that she would want me to call. The same throbbing pulse that I mentioned earlier was probably noticeable as I was dialing Lawrence's clinic.

"Lawrence and Phillips Pediatrics, can you please hold a moment?" Cindy greeted. We all knew each other from the same HMO Medical Group.

"Cindy, it's Danny Dawson."

"Danny Dawson. Now, why are you calling at a time when I can't chit chat?" she joked.

"I'm in kind of an urgent spot, actually. Is Dr. Lawrence available?"

"She's in do'n a physical – hold on, Danny."

I could hear her trying to get someone's attention that must have been passing by, "Wendy. Wendy! Knock on 5 and tell Anita that Dawson needs to speak with her about a patient. Dawson, you hold a minute and I'm sure she'll be right with you, alright?"

I really appreciated having support staff back in the HMO days.

"You take care of me and I'm not even in the same building anymore."

"Well, I heard Anita was want'n you about something yesterday. Did she try getting a hold of you?" Cindy asked.

"No," I replied.

I heard a familiar voice in the background before Cindy relayed, "Bill says to say hello."

"Dr. Winston's over there? Tell him the Dolphins still stink."

Cindy was a pro at these three-way conversations.

"Yeah, he's here only half the week. He doesn't have to work hard like you and me, Danny. I tell him he's a bum. Bill, Danny says to tell you the Dolphins ... There's Anita. Danny she's gonna pick up."

"Cindy, thanks," I said.

How funny to hear Dr. Winston's voice before being placed on hold. "Dawson said what about my Dolphins? What did he say?"

The line was silent for only a few seconds.

"Tell me you're calling about Sherry Gilland," Dr. Lawrence broached.

"Dr. Lawrence, you couldn't have started the conversation any better."

I was so relieved to hear her say Sherry's name. I wasn't sure how this was going to work given that I didn't have consent from Schultz. Dr. Lawrence has no inhibitions when it comes to parent opinions.

"This guy's creepy, don't you think?"

"We're talking about Joe?" I asked.

67

"Yeah, Joe. Joe…Schultz, I think. Isn't that right?

"That's Sherry's biological father," I confirmed.

"Do you ever talk with June or Skip?" she asked.

"It's not easy to get Sherry and June together, but yeah, I keep in touch with her. I'm not supposed to talk with Skip, though," I shared.

"What do you think's going on?" she paused "Sherry's not look'n happy at all to me."

"There's some heart breaking stuff happening but I'm trying to follow up on June's message that she left a moment ago. She's saying that Sherry has blood in her urine?"

"She does," Lawrence said "Let me read my note from yesterday. I have it here, let's see…." I could hear paper slapping. "She's complaining of back pain in middle - blood in urine - urine dark - had soiled underwear - pain going up steps and pain getting worse according to patient's report - lower abdominal pain - stool in peritenial area – erythema of vaginal opening - UA trace blood 3+ level – positive UTI," she paused before adding her recommendations, "and then I have Vaginosis Tub soak bid and Suprax 300mg."

"I don't do 'benefit of the doubt' on things like this but how possible is it that since he hasn't been a parent for very long that this is a hygiene issue?" I asked.

"The thing is, Danny, it was only last year that we gave him literature on various irritants like fabric softeners and detergents. So, from the past situation with the court…"

"Did anyone over there file a report?" I asked.

"No," she answered "They've already got an open case on this, don't they?"

"That's where I got the case but I don't know much because his attorney discourages him from signing releases. Like right now I don't know who's treating her because he fired me."

"Does he have the authority to do that? Who's looking after this acuity right now?" Lawrence asked.

"I'm going to call them right now. All this information goes beyond suspect," I said.

"I agree, Danny. What about those parent directors, I thought she had someone assigned by the court."

"The parent coordinator, from what I can tell, remains to be Rene Black." I said.

"Right…coordinator, that's what I meant. And Rene was really involved but I guess June simply couldn't afford her private practice fees. That doesn't seem right, either. A mother ought to be able to get assistance if it's being mandated by the court."

"I have a statute here that speaks about that very topic. Something really nuts is going on."

"This guy seems to have something on June and Skip. He's been getting the upper hand from the very beginning," she said. "I'm really glad you called. Tell you what, I'll have Cindy fax over my notes right away," she offered.

I immediately called DSS and spoke with a social worker after concluding my conversation with Lawrence. As my report was being taken, I can recall reading Dr. Lawrence's notes printing from my fax machine. The social worker was thorough. She even listened to the grave concerns I had about the pattern of cases that had family court involvement in common and how they are not accepted for investigation by DSS.

"Oh, it'll get accepted," she explained, "because the family is already known to the system. We're obligated by state law to investigate those."

"I understand that but it's not happening," I clarified.

Actually, I couldn't have felt more relief. I followed up with June before starting to clean up my copying mess. The office sounded like Grand Central that afternoon. I was surprised to pick up the next call and hear Schultz's voice.

"This is Danny."

"This is Joe Schultz," he said.

"What can I do for you, Mr. Schultz?"

"Darla told me that you're not willing to release Sherry's record. Is that true?" he asked.

"No, that's not true," was a half truth. "I can send the designated medical record, just not the psychotherapy notes."

"How about your billing records, too. There's a lot of stuff that needs to be cleared up," he announced.

"My billing? Do you need an updated statement?"

"No, I don't want an updated statement. I want the complete billing from the private pay and from the clinic. I want the complete chart. When can I expect to see it?"

In time, I thought to myself.

"As soon as we can align services through a new provider, Mr. Schultz."

"You don't have anything to do with my child's treatment anymore," he insisted.

"Mr. Schultz, I explained my concerns about depression and anxiety and I am recommending…"

He interrupted with a bullhorn voice, "I'LL BE THE ONE MAKING DECISIONS ON WHO SHE SEES. ME, JOE SCHULTZ, NOT YOU, DANNY DAWSON."

I didn't reply. I just waited silently. Something told me he wasn't in the mood to hear about privacy laws and ethics.

"And June just sent me an email say'n she's got another appointment scheduled for next week. Somehow she thinks she's gonna bring Sherry to see you," he said

Again, I said nothing. My tongue was starting to hurt.

"Hello?" he checked

"I'm still here, Mr. Schultz. She needs a psychiatrist – she needs a mental health provider."

"Well, anyway, that would be a violation of the court order. So, I'd think about that before keeping the appointment."

"I'll keep it in mind," I said.

"Back to the billing," he directed. "I saved you some time and went ahead and filed some dates with SocialWell" he said.

"You filed dates with SocialWell?"

"You know what I'm talking about. Sessions, therapy session dates," as if I should feel grateful for his assistance.

I was really confused because the only sessions filed with SocialWell were the ones at the clinic. My contract was terminated and the case was discussed with SocialWell before starting treatment in my private practice setting.

"You mean for sessions after the clinic closed?" I continued to fan my way through the billowing nonsense.

"Yeah. It's essentially leftover money, but cash it when it comes. It's yours," he awarded

"Leftover money? Joe, I'm not getting this," keeping my words close enough together to prevent his interruption, "but I'll definitely have a look over the Explanation of Benefit if it arrives."

"You do that," he poked, "and from here on out, remember to leave my daughter's treatment to me."

A series of emergency vehicles happened to be passing by on the street outside my window. I took a moment away from Schultz by drifting on the crescendo and decrescendo of sirens. I could still hear him but the receiver was half a foot from my ear.

"You acted outside of your role," he declared, "and you involved too many people."

My reply had a very exhaustive feel, "I need you to know that I did that again today, I think."

"What the hell are you talking about?" he snapped.

"I explained at our last meeting that Sherry's symptoms of anxiety and depression were worsening and I'm hoping DSS can help facilitate a new therapist. I contacted them earlier today after hearing that Sherry had blood in her urine, Joe."

Joe hung up on me. Surely, it was a natural response that he race to the nearest commode.

In response to June's email earlier:

From: Darla Tenor
To: June Gilland
 The order requires you and Joe to use someone covered by Joe's insurance.
 It is my understanding Joe has provided you with a list. I will ask him to forward you one again. Let him know who on the list you would like to use.
 In the meantime, if you would like to discuss minor changes to the custodial schedule or scheduling issues, the parent

coordinator is Rene Black. We believe you can afford to pay for meetings with Rene. She is able to communicate about the court order. Also, Rene's position does not require visits with Sherry nor is it appropriate in her role as parent coordinator.

It is inappropriate for you to talk to Judge Klein outside of court. Danny Dawson apparently feels he can contact people, too. If you have sent something to her you are obligated to provide me with a copy.

A few days later, June left another voice mail. She reminded me of how upset Schultz was about my filing the report. She was now "worried sick about Sherry's safety." June sounded horrified in her announcement: "I got DSS's notification letter – they didn't accept your report for investigation."

XI. Department of Selective Services

M y hand met the office phone as soon as I heard the message. "Department of child protection," was unfortunately a familiar greeting through the receiver.

"My name is Danny Dawson. I am calling for Mimi Frost regarding a report that I filed last week." My heart was throbbing up into my neck muscles.

"Did you not receive a letter?"

"That's why I'm calling; the report wasn't accepted for investigation but Mimi Frost said something about...."

"Sir, do you want to appeal the department's decision?"

"I want to talk with Mimi Frost," I repeated. "I was about to explain, she informed me that cases with prior reports are automatically accepted for...."

I tried to listen to myself about staying calm and took a breath.

"Sir, I can't put you through if a decision has been made. She is no longer assigned to the case if a letter was sent. The formal process would involve your request for an appeal."

I had a vision of Bronson's face come over me. Dr. Jordan Bronson is a psychologist that I worked with at a managed care facility ten years ago. It was only three months ago that I brought several of my clinicians to Social Services where we had a chance to present cases like this one.

"How about Bronson?" again slowing myself down "I'm sorry, Dr. Bronson. Is the director available?" I asked.

"Please hold," she replied.

After about two minutes, the line began ringing. I figured I would be looped back to the receptionist but the Dr. was indeed going to take my call.

"Hey, Dan. What can I do you for?" he sounded like he was having a pleasant day.

"Dr. Bronson, at the moment I am practicing my progressive relaxation skills. I'm again at a loss about your criteria for accepting reports," I said.

"It's not my criteria, it's the state's. Remember, there's no law saying you can't be a bad parent. We'd be investigating every little...."

It's my turn to be rude and interrupt. As the youngest of five, I didn't feel comfortable questioning my elders – but for better or worse, the awkwardness was getting easier to cope with.

"The cases I presented weren't about good parent – bad parent, it was about assessed child maltreatment."

"Dan, you know I'll do whatever I can. I'd be glad to take a look at the case," he offered.

"All right. How long will it take you? Because this one's high risk, too."

"I assume you've already received a letter from us?"

"That's why I'm calling, yes."

"You want to appeal then, and I can take care of that," he said. "This case was open in Deer County and somehow was transferred over to Hoffman County.

"Yeah, yeah, I remember you asking about jurisdiction matters. 'Same case?" he recalled.

"It's the same case except I've talked with her pediatrician and we're concerned about recurring vaginitis after the child started a new primary residence with her biological father. It was a very abrupt change. Letters from previous psychologists in Deer County spelled out some grave cautionary statements that were somehow rejected by the court. The child has told her mom and myself there was digital penetration perpetrated by bio dad."

"Geez, Dan. I'm really sorry to hear that," he sounded sincere. "Those custody cases are so complicated. Everyone's in such a vindictive headlock and usually the child is the last one considered."

I was amazed at how calm his voice was. I think he's able to dissociate because he kept ricocheting my questions to online statutes or just making more empathetic generalizations.

"Can you get someone to interview her now? Today?" I pleaded.

"Dan, it's a case by case basis around here. Who was the caseworker?" he asked.

"Mimi Frost. She took a complete history. No issues there, I'm not criticizing her role in this."

"Yeah, she's a veteran player around here," he said.

My tone may have broken a professional threshold, "It's probably not the individual social worker and it's not even the statutes. I've been looking at those too closely and I think they're well written. It's implementing what's written."

His chuckling accented his sentence, "That's pretty good, Dan. Can you be specific?"

Referencing my late night highlights I said, "Chapter Seven, Protective Services Section. That's the one you talked with us about a few months back. Remember telling me about the state mandated Structured Intake process?" I shook salt on his bleeding brain.

"Dan, I'm plenty familiar with it," his tone was more serious, "but the report wasn't accepted.

"But the 'Intake Safety Assessment' is in this same section," I challenged.

"And we've likely determined that there isn't any imminent harm to the child."

I was wondering if he was testing to see whether I had the information in front of me or if he didn't take time to read it himself. I was leading him to the prize language and, at this point, he knew it.

"And your department would rule out imminent harm according to...?"

And with one final sidestep response, Dr. Bronson postured himself front and center.

"Well, according to the definitions found in that same section."

My index finder was cemented to the definitions – I was ready.

"Both 'harm' and 'protective capacity' are defined very well and both apply to these cases, Jordan."

I think his wheels started to spin. "From the sound of it, you've got the statutes right there in front of you so go ahead and read how 'protective capacity' is defined for me."

Being candid could only help, "I do have it here" I said "Protective capacity refers to parenting skills, attachment to the child, awareness of and ability to interpret the child's needs and the adult's motivation to nurture the child. Harm is right next to it, if you'd like me to read that one, too."

"Dan, I'm going to look into the case for you. I can't promise much when you're essentially asking us to review a judge's order." With that, he stepped out of front and center where the focus was much less clear.

"Then that explains things." I rounded up. "If a judge is involved, you guys have to defer to the court's ruling?"

"That's not what I said, Dan."

The inner voice that usually coached calmness was at third base wind-milling me home.

"I think it's a 'read between the lines' thing, Jordan. Abuse happens at any time of the day or night. How's it possible for you guys to contact a judge at one o'clock in the morning about custody rights? Or is it that you're saying the judge doesn't want to feel like they screwed up by putting custody rights in the hands of a perp?"

Bronson told me to hold for a moment and I could hear the click of a door close quietly. The receiver ruffled for a long pause followed by his cryptic statement, "Things've been different ever since the Ochio case. I don't know if you're familiar with that or not."

"No, I'm not" I said.

"Take a look at it when you get a chance," more online referencing, "because the lower court trusted DSS workers when they asked for orders to enter the home up until that point."

That may in fact be true but it all sounded like diversion mastery when a child was in harm's way in the here and now. All I could do was document, document, document.

XII. Social Well

An email is sent and a letter is opened. Today's mail included the award check of leftover money from SocialWell that Schultz had alerted me was in route. I really didn't believe it but desensitization was taking the element out of surprise out of most experiences lately.

The document that arrived is called an Explanation of Benefit. When a provider submits a medical claim, a CPT code (Current Procedural Terminology) is required. It's a five digit number that specifies the type of service provided to the patient. If and when the insurance pays the provider, the check is accompanied by an Explanation of Benefit. This is a form which is basically a receipt used to help track and reconcile patient accounts. I really didn't think he was serious when he told me SocialWell was sending me a check. There was no way I could see an insurance company sending money without first having this kind of information. Here before my eyes was a check made payable to me in the amount of 263.63 dollars. The envelope was on my desk but I flipped it over to examine the return address. It sure looked like it was for real. I sat down and began looking over the dates of service but immediately noticed there were no CPT codes. Also, the amounts were different for each the three dates of service listed.

The letterhead included a phone number so I thought I'd attempt to get an explanation of the Explanation. Are you still with me?

"That's not something we would do. Claims are processed only after authorization is obtained. I can transfer you to authorizations and you can certainly ask them to back date your claim but there's no guarantee of payment in situations like that. Do you have any further questions before I transfer you?" the voice asked.

"No, no. What I'm saying is a check was sent to me. I have it in my hand right now" I waved the letter in the air as if I was on Skype. "The member alerted me that he filed dates of service. One of these never happened and the other two have different amounts but no description of the service provided. He's already paid me so I know it's not my money."

"And you're saying you didn't even file it with us?" she asked.

"That's correct. I terminated my contract with SocialWell about seven months ago," I replied.

"Well, if in fact the check you're holding was processed by SocialWell, I've never heard of that happening before. There should be something on it, there should be at least a check number," she said.

"I've got it. It's check number 7324177.""

"Very strange," the voice sounded still skeptical. "I'll have to take your information and have someone get back to you."

I made copies of everything and then sent the check back with a brief explanation:

This letter serves to document that the dates of service reported on check number 7324177 are incorrect. This can also reflect that the reported service dates and respective discrepancies (listed under "Billed") originated from the member.

CC: Schultz

Several days after mailing the check back, SocialWell returned my call. I was anticipating some kind of "Thank you for calling this to our attention, Sir" or something along those lines. Instead, they were calling to tell me I was in violation of my provider contract – one of the nine insurance contracts terminated as part of closing formal business operations at the clinic.

"This is Nancy Baggot calling from SocialWell Insurance Company in Chicago Illinois. I am calling on behalf of our member Sherry Gilland."

"Do you have a release?" I asked.

"Just one moment, please" she replied.

I could hear quiet consultation followed by a rapid clicking sound before being placed on the speaker phone.

"Mr. Dawson, can you hear me okay?" It was Nancy's consultant stepping out from behind the curtain.

"Yes," I answered.

"My name is Alissa Rechit. I'm the Network Services Director for SocialWell. Our member states that you've been charging him out of pocket when there's a contracted fee schedule in place. He should only be paying a copayment of $6.60."

"Ms. Rechit, this is an absolute mind blower," I leaned back and stared wide-eyed at my office ceiling. A trance of words slid from my mouth, "My contract was terminated in November of last year."

"No," she said. "You can't terminate this contract so long as you're seeing one of our members."

"SocialWell sent me the acknowledgement letter in November. Doesn't that count for anything?" I asked.

There was no answer but I knew they were still on the line – someone had a nasty cough.

Reality testing resumed, "You're saying the only way out of your provider contract is if I what, if I stop practicing? How about if I died?"

That may have stumped her, "I don't know what to tell you. But your situation doesn't release you from treating our member according to the fee schedule that was originally signed.

"Mr. Dawson, I know this contract like the back of my hand," she asserted, "and I don't have time to debate this any longer. If you'd like to talk with our legal counsel instead of working this out with me, that's fine. What I'm trying to tell you is that our member needs to be reimbursed. Either you can write him a check directly or you can write SocialWell a check and we'll reimburse the member."

"Write you a check?" I was at the edge of my chair "For what?"

"He has receipts reflecting these out of pocket payments for the past, let me see…" I could hear papers shuffling but, to me, it sounded more like being rung up for a week's worth of groceries "…looks like weekly for at least the past five months. So it would be the difference between his copayment and your…."

I interrupted, "That's impossible, unless he forged receipts. I'm still confused about contract termination procedures but that's probably the best place to start. Have you seen any of these receipts?"

Ms. Rechit's heavy sighs reminded me of recent communications with Tenor. "No, I have not. I'll be glad to get those and fax them to you but I expect payment immediately after you've reviewed them. This can't go on forever."

I knew there wasn't going to be any legitimate receipts but still was baffled about why SocialWell was so fixed on my being at fault. I just figured someone among the higher ups would perhaps instruct employees such as Alissa Rechit to consider the psychological makeup of their own clientele when situations like this arise. Whether Schultz is or isn't mentally ill, we all know that it can run through a family's DNA. I was waiting for any hints of her having communication with Tenor.

"Okay, but before hanging up I wanted to clarify a couple of things." I was looking for scratch paper so I could document her answers along with the time and date of our conversation. "Did you happen to receive a returned check in recent days from me?"

Both Alissa and Nancy quickly convened, "No. There's no record of that in the database here."

I imagined them watching it go through a shredder. "It would be great if you could look over the explanation of benefit that was attached to that check or I can fax a copy of it if it doesn't show up. The other document to review before we talk again is her most recent assessment and whether or not she is receiving treatment. This young girl is severely depressed and, as it reads in my recommendation, needs to be assigned to a new provider as soon as possible. She really needs to get in with a psychiatrist."

"Look, Mr. Dawson, maybe it's best you just talk with our legal counsel. We have a duty to get our member his money back and, from the sounds of it, you're not going to help us do that," Rechit said.

"Wouldn't you want to understand exactly how much and for what you're writing a check for? This is hundreds of dollars we're talk'n about, Ms. Rechit."

"I'd pay it back before I had legal problems, but that's me," both seemed to find that humorous.

I laid my forehead on the edge of my desk, "Then go ahead and have your legal counsel contact me, I guess."

To my surprise, she showed pity by offering another chance. "I'm willing to work through this with you. I just need to know that you're going to pay the money back when you get these receipts."

There was a stinky breeze coming from her mouth. I was now interested in whether she took this on by herself or if she was truly backing the company's policy and procedures.

"Nah, I think you're right. Let's go ahead and move this forward to the next step. There are too many perplexing things about how SocialWell is doing business here. I don't think an owner would be too happy to know that checks are being cut to providers for services that never happened."

I heard Nancy say, "What's he referring to?" but Alissa took out the slack, "I'll give your name to our counsel if that's what you want, then."

The call never came but the open ended anticipation was more than I could digest. My follow up conversation with SocialWell's attorney was surprisingly quite pleasant. Given the fact that I spent time in Chicago as a kid, we struck up conversation pretty easily. He felt so comfortable that he started telling me all about his current family situation. He was questioning his current wife's assessment of his stepson's behavior. The question he wanted answered from me was if behavior could be purely related to the stepson's OCD or if it would be possible that he was acting out because of religious differences. Apparently, his wife is Jewish and he is Protestant. I shared my great wisdom from years of experience working with children and families: I told him I had no clue. Once he realized the limitations of the consultation, we were onto the business.

He knew nothing about the situation and informed me that he was the only attorney on SocialWell's payroll. He was particularly interested in the check I returned and planned to investigate what he believed "sounded pretty fishy." He opened a database while on the phone with me and, unbeknownst to him, started singing lyrics I was longing to hear. He said, "Member's attorney, Darla Tenor, calling about dates of service – upset about member being double billed and requesting letter from SocialWell for the purpose of upcoming court hearing - billing fraud."

I was temporarily pacified with his verbal agreement to draft a letter stating there was no contract violation and no outstanding balance owed. He then offered his own professional summary "...not to dismiss what appears to be our own possible oversights but at the same time it sounds to me like this guy's attorney has it out for you. You didn't take her bait and cash the check so she's taking a different approach. You've got your hands full with this one, don't you?"

This would turn out to be my final correspondence with SocialWell. However, it wasn't until my open court testimony that I realized SocialWell was the one struggling to break free of Tenor's hooks.

XIII. Your Honor

Entering the front doors of the court house, the first objective was getting through a long line at the security check-in. The line was slow moving, plenty of time for me to pinpoint words 'Case Coordinators/Domestic' on the directory. Elevator up...I was needing a face to face with the wizard.

A rectangular lobby was surrounded by small offices. I decided to arbitrarily approach one with an open door. Just as I stepped over the threshold, a voice from over my left shoulder stopped me.

"Is there something I can help you find?"

I turned to find a middle aged man who had all the gadgets of a janitor.

"Maybe you can," I accepted. "I'm looking for Judge Klein's case coordinator."

He turned and pointed directly across the center of the lobby "That would be Janet Evans."

He bent backwards slightly at the waist to get an unobstructed view, "Looks like she's on the phone but if you'll have a seat I'll be glad to tell her there's someone waiting."

Nice guy. Maybe it's not as bad as I think. I wasn't in the chair two minutes before the wizard's assistant introduced herself.

"I'm Janet Evans. Can I help you?" she asked.

I stood up to shake her hand. She had a warm smile and seemed like she was going to be easy enough to work with.

"I'm really hoping you can," I replied.

"I have grave concern about the welfare of a child on one of Judge Klein's custody cases,"

"Is the parent with you?" she asked.

"I wasn't sure if I would need the parent to accompany me or not," I waited, "so we can't talk at all?"

I put my hand on my forehead before seeking further advice.

"How do you handle situation where suspected abuse is occurring in the child's primary residence?" I asked.

"You mean now or in the past?"

"Now," I answered.

"I'd contact DSS," she said, "but come on in my office and I'll get the case number. Judge Klein would at least want a message."

I followed her into a small office fitted with a large desk and several filing cabinets.

"Have a seat," she climbed into her desk chair like it was a cockpit.

Her headset was connected "What's the child's name?" she asked

"The last name is Gilland," I said. She happened to be looking at the paper but then quickly looked up at me.

She put her pen down and reached for her headset.

"How are you involved in this case again?" she asked.

"I'm the court appointed therapist," I answered. "Is there something wrong?"

She was adjusting the headset microphone.

"No problem," she responded. "What's the specifics of your concern? You believe she's being abused?"

"She's reporting sexual abuse and I have medical notes from her pediatrician that are supporting the same. It's beyond a 'suspect' threshold, that's for damn sure."

Somehow, Evans managed to call Klein without dialing. She held her index finger up to signal silence.

Evans relayed, "Judge Klein, there's a Danny Dawson here that has concern about the child in the Schultz vs Gilland case. He's here after apparently getting reports of abuse including some medical records."

Evans looked at me, "Did you contact social services already?"

"Yes. The case wasn't accepted for investigation," I said.

Evans was fielding what seemed to be continual questions but also trying to understand my responses.

"I'll make sure, he's right here." She looked directly at me, "If this is an emergency, you need to contact DSS."

I had a frustrated smirk, "The emergent status was received as less than urgent by DSS. They are not going to interview Sherry. That's why I'm here. I spoke directly with the Director of Child Protection" I explained.

Evans said something that I couldn't make out and then took her headset off and laid it on the desk.

"I'll be right back," Evans said, "her office isn't far down the hall here."

After about five minutes, she returned. She sat down again and said," Judge Klein can possibly meet with you in the court room at 3:00 P.M. after court concludes," she offered. "Keep in mind both parties will need to be present or at least have representation in order for this to happen."

I had already cancelled three families this morning, and this would mean canceling another two this afternoon.

"How soon before we'll know about whether people are going to be able to be here or not?"

Evans swiveled to her computer screen. "I can send emails and make calls right now," she said.

"Great. Thanks for doing this," I said.

"No problem. Why don't you have a seat back out there and as soon as I know something I'll let you know" she said.

I was quite impressed to hear Evan's confirmation; we were set to meet The Great Oz. I looked at my watch and said to myself, "Wow. Only about one football game away and I'll know what's going on." How immature, eh? Measuring time in terms of a football game.

I entered the court room and immediately spotted June in the front row.

"Hey," I greeted June.

"Hey," she said "Gilland's in the back, did you see him?"

"Skip's here?" I turned and saw him in the far back row. He put his hand up and wiggled his fingers. The more I learned about him, the more I learned about his compassion. He deeply loves June and Sherry. "Great. Glad to see him here."

June looked straight ahead where the bailiff and court reporter stood. Just to the right were two city police officers.

"Really great," she said sarcastically. "See those cops? There's two more along with a sheriff that's been following Skip and I from the second we stepped foot in the building."

"Don't sweat it," I said without knowing what I was dismissing. "Even if they are here for him, what did he do wrong? Doesn't the public have a right to be in these hearings?"

"They can do whatever they feel like doing," she said.

Judge Klein entered from a side door and got started immediately.

"First of all, what exactly are we doing here, Mr. Dawson," she wore black-framed bifocal glasses. She didn't bother looking up from whatever papers were in front of her.

"Thank you, Your Honor, for hearing me today," I attempted to begin answering her question.

"Well, I don't know that you're going to be able to be heard" she remarked "We are here only if the parties consent, otherwise, I have no ability to hear any matters when there's no motion standing before the court or anything brought to the court specifically by one of the parties."

"I approached your case coordinator this morning but didn't realize it would require all of us to meet in open court. I appreciate...." I was interrupted again.

"Ahhh, yes, you did," she stretched. "This isn't the first time you've attempted to contact me. You attempted to contact me on a prior occasion and I believe I returned that phone message and indicated to you at that time that I could not contact or communicate with you without both parties being present and without both of their consent."

No big deal, she's a lying judge. What a feeling to sit in front of a judge and know that she knows that you know she's lying. At forty, I was just beginning to see the light cracking through a thick haze of naiveté. Klein was referencing a cover letter that accompanied a child's mental health record from one of my clinicians. A different case but loaded with the same kind family court tampering. If her intent was to christen our meeting with intimidation, it was effective. She was letting me know from the start of this meeting that she did in fact get my messages about HIPAA regulations and other specifics pertaining to the release of a minor's record. She didn't respond because she doesn't have to. Klein was in the center of the web, reminding me of my actions from the recent past and how sticky my limbs must be getting right about now.

I didn't know the half of it.

"I don't recall receiving that message, your honor," I hope my eye twitch wasn't too obvious each time I had to say "your honor." "As you know, I was in your case coordinator's office this morning. She was speaking with you about scheduling this meeting." I held my right arm out toward Ms. Tenor, "I'm grateful that she was able to contact the parties and the parties were able to be present on such short notice." The court transcript was a blessing.

"Okay, okay." Klein didn't like where that was going apparently. "So I'm somewhat at a loss as to why we are here and frankly the information you gave to my case coordinator indicates that this child is in physical danger. You need to contact DSS if that's the case."

From this point, it's dreamy. If the following doesn't seem fluent, don't bother adjusting your antenna because the picture isn't going to get much clearer. She kept catapulting redundancies.

"I filed a report with DSS and also...."

Klein was obviously preoccupied with something else.

"So, arrangements had to be made in contacting Ms. Tenor's office but I'm not quite sure how Ms. Gilland got news of your attempt to contact me today."

Ms. Evans wasn't here to stand up. I don't know that she would even if she were here. I'm so glad I was able to review this on the transcript. It's anchor to reality for me. I wasn't sure if I was imagining the whole experience or if I really asked the judge for help.

"Was June not supposed to be contacted? I think June thinks she's one of the parties."

"Hold just a sec," June prompted "I got news about this meeting from Janet Evans. I printed the email, it's right here." June leaned down for her purse.

"I was not aware of that," she looked to the side for a moment "Then I guess that answers that, doesn't it."

87

That was Cruella Deville talking about the Dalmatian puppies. Sure enough, Janet Evans was coincidentally fired shortly after this meeting. I believe she knew what she was doing. Janet was on this case from the minute jurisdiction was mysteriously changed. If you're reading this Janet, thanks.

"Your honor, I am here because the child's medical records indicate that she has blood in her urine and she is reporting sexual abuse, perpetrated by Mr. Schultz," I said.

"Is this from your own personal knowledge?" she stalled.

"From my independent interview with Sherry, collateral conversations with her mother, as well as Sherry's pediatrician."

"Is the pediatrician here today?" Klein looked over her glasses for any raised hands.

"No. I don't believe she is here," I said.

Off came the glasses, and the gloves for that matter.

"Well and that may be the case, Sir, but that has to be the subject of a hearing after proper notice and the opportunity for witnesses to be contacted because there is a court order in place," Klein dictated.

"I have become aware of misrepresentations in the court order...."

My air time was getting lower as her level of agitation got higher.

"That may be the case but this can only be heard after proper notice with rather than simply you know, if this is an emergency, then report it to the appropriate authorities. Don't attempt a communication in here," she glared.

"Your Honor, the misrepresentations have obstructed services for this child. It seems there is information from other providers and DSS that...."

I wasn't going to talk over the judge when she cut me off

"Then it sounds to me as if you need to testify about matters that have been already heard," her voice was suddenly much louder as the anger climbed to a rolling boil. "The problem we're having is there is no pending motion before this court."

I didn't want to assume responsibility for inappropriate communication with the court. Again, I was thinking of the audio transcript.

"I was following the guidance of your case coordinator. This was a scheduled meeting, your Honor."

Darla covered her mouth like a kid does when a sibling gets in trouble by the parent. "Are we finished, your Honor? Or," motioning to me, "does the jury have more to share?"

"I'm only trying to communicate the situation as it stands right now," I reiterated.

"Then file the appropriate motion," Klein scolded me.

June referenced multiple attempts in the past. "Your Honor, I've tried filing an exparte and ..."

Klein can be heard exploding with anger.

"Here's the problem," pointing at me, "he is not your lawyer!"

June held her head down. Her financial hardships didn't allow representation any longer.

Klein's threshold was fast approaching, implosion was imminent. Firing from the fringe, she revealed a weapon that was waiting in the wings.

"Ms. Tenor, do you have something you'd care to introduce at this time?" Klein announced.

Darla pulled a single sheet from under several soft-cover folders. She stood up and approached Klein with the document. "I do, Your Honor." Half way back to her seat, Darla released the safety. A confident calm came over her presentation as crosshairs were locked onto my career.

"From my understanding at this point, Mr. Dawson is under investigation for double billing Mr. Schultz," she was blowing smoke from the barrel before sitting down.

"Isn't double billing a nice way of saying fraud?" Klein snorted with the bailiff.

"I haven't received anything from my board saying that," I said.

Klein displayed the document as if it were show and tell. "It's addressed to you," she said with an accusatory tone. "Do you read your mail?"

"Yes I do, Your Honor.

"Then take a look at this, maybe it'll jog your memory.

SOCIALWELL

Dear Mr. Dawson,

This letter is to notify you of an over-payment on behalf of the above referenced client. During our audit of the claims it was determined that SocialWell and the Member both reimbursed you for services rendered.

SocialWell is requesting that you reimburse the Plan the amount of $653.40. The payment should be made to SocialWell. Once this payment is received, the account for this case will be closed.

If you have any questions regarding the payment, please feel free to contact me.

Sam L. Bell, MSW
Sr. VP Quality Management

Cc: Member

Even with the old clinic address, I would've received this document if it were mailed because I continued to receive all my other forwarding mail.

"I notice that it has my old address but still think I should've received it. I've honestly never seen this before," I said.

"Sounds serious…are you continuing to practice – let me rephrase that, are you continuing to see Sherry?" Klein asked.

(I'll take 'subtle extortion' for $500)

Darla's excitability came out in jumbled words "He is not her father's therapist. He's been fired."

"By Mr. Schultz, not by me" June said.

It's a miracle that I have the following question on the transcript: "Does he have the authority to do that, Your Honor?"

Klein spoke through her teeth and looked me directly in the eyes, "I don't know about that. I'll have to look into it but you may not represent her."

Klein pointed down at me, "You went into my case coordinator's office and it sounds to me based on what Ms. Gilland is saying that you must've alerted her to this meeting. Is that right? Did Mr. Dawson contact you about this meeting today, Ms. Gilland?"

"I am allowed to communicate with Mr. Dawson," June asserted.

At that moment, a secret signal must have been given because several officers began walking to the back of the courtroom toward Skip Gilland.

One either side of Skip, they began escorting him from the court room pew. "And Mr. Gilland obviously gets to communicate with you also." Off with the glasses again before directing her anger to the back of the court room. "Mr. Gilland, you need to leave the court room. You are not a party to this action and you are not welcome at any of these proceedings." Through the teeth again, "I'm going to tell you for the last time, you are not a party to this action and you are asked to not come to these meetings again."

Driving out of the parking garage, my cell started ringing. I didn't recognize the number but took the call since I'd been out of the office.

"This is Danny,"

"Danny, it's Darla Tenor. Would you mind telling me what you're still doing on this case," she growled.

"Sherry needs treatment ASAP," I said.

"That's all well and good, Mr. Dawson, but she is no longer your patient. Joe Schultz fired you," she said.

"I need a date and name of the new therapist before I can close this case. There are too many high risk issues. I'd be abandoning her."

Klein must have let the entire cast have it after we left the court house.

"Let me tell you what you're actually doing, Mr. Dawson. You're alienating yourself and by contacting Judge Klein, you're acting unethical," she threatened.

"I'll take that risk," I said.

She laughed, "You need to provide my client with the original chart and then keep yourself under control, Sir." She paused. "By the time I return to the office next Monday, I intend on having your compliance. You're beginning to bring on quite a bit of trouble for yourself," she threatened.

I was now merging onto a busy street that led traffic out of the city. I really couldn't focus on talking anyway. But she managed to cram a lot of creepiness in just one or two sentences.

"You have no idea, Mr. Dawson" Darla said "I thought after your talk with DSS and surely after today's informative meeting with Judge Klein you'd understand that you're way in above your head."

However, the content of my report could only be verified through court transcripts so I felt compelled to send a certified follow up letter with all the important topics discussed that day. I received the following letter only days later:

Dear Mr. Danny Dawson

I have received your letter addressed to Judge Klein. I am returning your letter to you unread by Judge Klein. The state's Code of Judicial Conduct prohibits judges from having ex parte communications with litigants (communications with one party without the other party/parties being present). Any copies of this letter placed in the file will be removed. Further attempts to influence the judge's decision through out of court contact will result in a report to the appropriate professional review boards.

Sincerely, Janet Evans
Domestic Case Coordinator
Cc: Darla Tenor

XIV. Under Investigation

B etween the letter from Klein's case coordinator threatening to
contact my licensure board and this SocialWell letter presented
in court, I thought I'd be proactive. I called the board hoping to gain
insight and advice on the complaint process. Most of the board
members and general support staff must've been enjoying summer
vacation because it was the executive director answering phones. Who
knows, maybe it was meant to be because her advice about handling
complaints was crystal clear:

"Get legal counsel."

Had I been standing in the room, she may have thought I had
swimmer's ear.

"You mean for myself, I should have legal representation?"

"That's right," she confirmed "But don't do anything right now,
nothing's been filed against you."

How could I possibly afford an attorney? I was trying to pay off
corporate loans I used for paying my clinicians. The Medicaid vendors
denied payment, so I had to cough up currency for my provider's
salary. What if I ended up having to pay an attorney like all of these
parents in family court? What if I had to pay retainers? I never knew
how people came up with $5,000 to "get started."

No worries – this kind of 'what if' thinking was short lived. The
complaint arrived about ten days later. The anticipation of getting mail
each day started giving me mouth sores. Over the next two years, my
wife and I developed simple trauma symptoms associated with pink
4x5 postcards. Of all the certified letters sent from the board, it
would've helped if we were home to sign for at least one or two. It was
agony to hold that card overnight, waiting until an exchange could be
made at the post office.

Here is the beginning of a very disturbing process – an injurious
regimen designed and implemented by governor-elected officials:
(Boards and Commissions office has no idea who oversees the conduct
of board members. Occupational Licensing Boards will often have a
democratic approach whereby licensees can vote for their board

members. The Clinical Social Work Board in this state however 'tells' the licensees who will be elected. I eventually met with the governor. Guess what? She said, "Not me. Off hand, I couldn't tell you who's appointing those members. That's ridiculous that you're being treated that way when you're defending the child's rights." She was definitely encouraging and affirming. So were the senators I met with, but nothing ever changed.)

COMPLAINT LETTER

The Board has received a complaint against you from Joseph Schultz alleging that you have violated the Social Work Certification/Licensure Act Ethical Guidelines. The board may assign an investigator to investigate this allegation. The assignment of an investigator should not be interpreted as an assumption that a violation has occurred. The completed report from the investigator will be submitted to the board and at that time a determination will be made as to whether there is sufficient evidence to proceed to hearing concerning a possible violation. An investigation into allegations of ethical misconduct follows no established timetable. We will expedite this matter and strive to complete the investigation in a timely manner. The process is facilitated by full cooperation with the investigator assigned by the board.

The complaints are listed under "Purpose and Scope", "Remuneration" Billing Fraud and "Confidentiality and Record Keeping." Schultz's statement of misconduct is under a category titled Purpose and Scope. It states: Danny Dawson violated the court order by calling an emergency meeting with Judge Klein that was not necessary." Okay. Maybe I can get some guidance on how to approach the system – that could only be helpful. Under Confidentiality and Record Keeping, Joe lists that I provided an activity calendar to June. I'm okay with that as well, especially given the language that encourages co-parenting and the sharing of information pertaining to extracurricular activities. The last one, Remuneration, Joe accuses me of billing fraud.

I wrestled with the idea of contacting an attorney but decided to wait until after my initial conversation with the assigned investigator, John Stafford. As much as I dreaded the entire matter, I couldn't wait for this initial meeting.

I cleared the office desk except for a few reference items, a pen and scratch pad. The call came ten minutes later than what we scheduled. Not a big deal but those ten minutes felt like three hours.

I answered, "This is Danny."

"Good afternoon, Mr. Dawson?" he asked.

"Yes."

"This is John Stafford," his voice was casual "I'm the assigned investigator to the case involving a complaint filed against you."

"Yes. Thank you for calling," was all that came to mind.

"This may take at least an hour. Depending on how long your responses are, it could perhaps last as long as an hour and a half or even two hours."

"The time is blocked so I don't expect any interruptions," I said.

How strange it was for him at that moment to put me on hold for another phone call.

"Dan, hold on. I need to take this call," he instructed.

So much for Mr. Dawson, I guess. Maybe, he doesn't realize that we're discussing my State License and that I've been thinking about this phone call from the minute it was scheduled.

"Are you still there?" the voice was so casual, just as slow and relaxed as can be

"Yes, Sir" I replied.

"Fine, then" Stafford cleared his throat "If you don't mind, let's start with what I believe is the most serious allegation and that would be the billing fraud."

A freezing steel rod hijacked my spine.

"I'm anxious to hear where this is coming from," I commented.

"It's actually spelled out quite clearly in the complaint letter that, I am presuming, you received some weeks back. Do you not have that in front of you?"

If he understands where billing fraud makes sense, I'm already at a disadvantage.

"Yes, I have the complaint letter in front of me" I said "but I don't see any specifics."

"What kind of specifics do you need?" he asked.

"Mr. Stafford, if I may ask a question since we've just started?" I felt like I was speaking with a court judge, not a social worker.

"Go right ahead," he said.

"I certainly can respect your opinion about the importance of the billing matter, but did you receive a copy of my written response about child protection issues and Sherry's need for continuing care – right now?" I politely asked.

"Yeah, yeah, yeah," he remarked. "I've read all the stuff about your problems with the state mental health reform and child protection if that's what you're referring to," he took a breath "what you need to start understanding is that billing fraud is serious. As far as I know she's fine and your career's on the line with this stuff."

The patronizing wasn't a bother simply because his credibility was weak. He had set a tone that was contrary to the core values of the profession. He was disregarding a colleague's professional opinion without having any direct knowledge of the case. A sickness grew inside of me as I looked around from inside of a Stephen King Snow Globe.

Could this really be a social worker on the other end of the phone or had they hired a poacher to handle this investigation?

Too, I thought to myself, there is the consideration that a majority of professional conduct allegations are indeed valid and worthy of appropriate discipline. Some of the stuff I hear about is more worthy of a disciplinary beating.

John Stafford, the board's investigator, had more to share. It was as if his objective in this initial meeting was to ensure that I get legal representation. But the conclusion of our conversation is important because it sets a tone for the board's conduct over the next thirty-one months of captivity.

"Tell you what," he swaggered, "let's talk about your belief that Mr. Schultz was planning to somehow become the child's Guardian ad

Litem so that they could leave the country. That certainly sounded strange, I agree."

"Mr. Stafford, this isn't information that is exclusive to my interactions with the family." I announced "This information is, in each and every circumstance, evidenced in various written communications, emails, letters, medical notes, things like this."

There was a half minute of silence, I wondered if he had become tiresome of my story and clicked over to another incoming call. I was mistaken. Mr. Stafford was taking a deep breath.

"No offense, but it doesn't sound like you're familiar with how the GAL role functions," he sneered "A court would never sign for someone like a parent, it would be biased."

I scrambled through my papers, "Sir, I can fax a copy of an application signed by the clerk of court."

"With Joe Schultz as the identified applicant, Mr. Dawson?"

"Yes, Sir. With Joe Schultz as the identified applicant."

Another long silence before he spoke.

"I'm asking for that and any proof about the insurance matter," he demanded. "We'll be speaking with SocialWell's attorney on Monday and I gotta tell you off record, I'd strongly consider retaining counsel."

On record, I was introduced to the Anderson and Burns Law Firm where I found a clear path to bankruptcy.

XV. Motion to Quash

Before retaining Gretchen Platt with Anderson and Burns, I was on a long quest for representation. I was sending emails on a daily basis, telling my story in a sales pitch fashion in hopes of getting assistance. No one wanted to take a short tour on the Titanic. During this time, I experienced a few interesting things. Here's one that reflects the infected ethics pervading the state.

You'll hear more about Foy Dillard, but for now, just keep in mind that he was running for a spot in the Senate during my board investigation. Of the many SOS emails sent, I had no idea Foy had a contractual arrangement with my licensure board when I sent one to his law firm. My inquiry was forwarded within his law firm but the inter-office reply was obviously not meant for my eyes:

> *"Please contact him and tell him that we are not interested in his case. I do NOT want to provide him a referral; also, do not tell him that we represent the SW board. The board does not want this to be public information. He can contact the Lawyers Referral Service."*

The response, meant for me, was sent by the owner of the firm, Randy Manson. Mr. Manson accidentally sat on the 'reply all' button and, inadvertently forwarded Foy's reply to me. Given his current campaign pride, Foy probably had a few involuntary movements after reading this one. When I think about the moment this email was written from Randy to Foy, I can't help visualizing Barney Fife holding up his holster and pecking at the keyboard with the other:

> Mr. Dawson, unfortunately, we cannot assist you. Our firm deals exclusively with immigration law. However, you may contact the 1-800 lawyer referral line.

There are a few key players mentioned in this book that could get together and author a book titled *Soft Money for Dummies*. Maybe it's a stretch, but my resistance seemed to be met with little pink index cards from the postmaster. Certified letters were either from the board or part of Tenor's paper trail of terror. Here's one from the latter:

Re: Sherry
Dear Danny,

It has come to the attention of Joe Schultz that you are continuing to treat Sherry Gilland despite the fact that Mr. Schultz, as the primary custodian of Sherry, terminated your services. In addition, Mr. Schultz has asked you to provide him with Sherry's original file, which you have refused to do.

Please cease all treatment of Sherry Gilland immediately so that she may begin therapy with a new therapist.

Sincerely yours,

Darla V. Tenor

I think cancer may sign letters in a similar way.

Darla Tenor has a prim disgust when she has to work in an open system. Mention the word 'continuity' and her back will arch. During the first several weeks after Schultz fired me, Darla was upset that I would not discontinue therapy until an identified provider took my place. I continued to emphasize that once an appointment was made, the original record and treatment summary would immediately follow.

If the story sounds like it's branching out, it's because I now had two separate issues with defense representation. I wasn't having any luck finding an attorney for my board complaint but I did get counsel regarding the record release issue.

Judy Crandall was a family law attorney. I recognized her name from at least one previous case. Judy contacted me and offered representation in protecting Sherry's record. Her advice was clear and affirming:

"I suggest you wait for Klein's order and then I'll file a motion to quash."

The order arrived a day or two later and Judy's motion to quash was quashed. And despite Darla's emphasis on the original files, it was a copy that was produced under seal to Judge Klein. After signing across the seal, I extended the envelope containing the complete confidential file. We both understood that Klein and Tenor would be pilfering through it within the hour.

STATE OF IN THE GENERAL COURT OF JUSTICE
HOFFMANN COUNTYDISTRICT COURT DIVISION

JUNE GILLAND
Plaintiff
v.
M MOTION TO QUASH
JOSEPH SCHULTZ
Defendant

The undersigned moves the Court pursuant to Rule 00(x) of the State Rules of Civil Procedure to quash a subpoena served on Danny Dawson in this matter and respectfully shows the Court:

1. A subpoena to produce and permit inspection was apparently issued and properly served on Danny Dawson. "Any and all reports, records, notes, and files regarding [a minor child]" whom Mr. Dawson has been treating in a patient-therapist relationship.
2. The subpoena fails to allow reasonable time for compliance.
3. The subpoena requires disclosure of privileged and otherwise protected matter, and no exception or waiver applies to the privilege or protection.
4. The subpoena is procedurally defective in that it does not permit sufficient time for responding; in that it does not appear to require production at a hearing or deposition; in that the undersigned cannot determine whether or not copies of the subpoena have been served upon all parties in the matter; and in that there does not

appear to be any matter pending before the court that warrants such a subpoena.

5. Upon information and belief, the court previously ordered that Mr. Dawson continue as the therapist for the minor child in this matter, but the defendant who issued the subpoena in question long ago fired Mr. Dawson and filed a complaint against Mr. Dawson with his licensing agency such that the subpoena appears to be issued for an improper purpose.

6. In this case, the defendant has previously issued a subpoena which required Mr. Dawson to file a motion to quash, and he issued a similar subpoena in a related case which also required Mr. Dawson to have representation to protect his confidential records.

WHEREFORE, the undersigned attorney prays the court to quash the subpoena and further prays that the court order the defendant, who issued the subpoena, to pay the reasonable expenses including attorney fees incurred by Mr. Dawson as a result of the issuance of the subpoena.

Judy Crandall
LAW OFFICE OF JUDY CRANDALL
Attorney for Danny Dawson

The following affidavit accompanied Sherry's record:

Danny Dawson, being first duly sworn, deposes and says:

I have filed a motion to quash a subpoena issued by the defendant in this action to produce my records regarding treatment of Sherry Gilland based upon a number of reasons, including concern for the child and my belief that disclosure is not in the child's best interest.

Sherry is experiencing depression and severe anxiety. She is extremely fearful of her father. She also fears disclosure to her father of her communications with me because she is afraid she will be "punished" if he knows what she has said. She believes that if her father learns what she is saying about her needs regarding her mother, he will be so angry he will do whatever he can to try to get her mother put in jail.

During the time I have been seeing Sherry, I have observed her anxiety increase and her depression become worse. She has lost weight, her eating and sleeping patterns are more disrupted. She has become less verbally communicative, and her drawings have become more disturbing, with morbid themes.

I am gravely concerned about Sherry's welfare, especially if her communications with me are not kept confidential.

Pursuant to the order of the Court, I am providing the presiding judge with a copy under seal of my complete file, which includes psychotherapy notes and clinical documentation as well as billing statements and reports.

I have never disclosed to anyone any of the psychotherapy notes, clinical documentation, or other therapeutic records. Billing statements and reports for the purpose of obtaining insurance have been provided to the appropriate parties to the extent necessary to obtain coverage as requested by the defendant. All of my files on this child have been included in the sealed envelope being delivered to the Judge.

Judy Crandall

Attorney for Danny Dawson

XVI. A Staged Arrest

June contacted me several months after Sherry's records were released to inform me that Klein had a warrant out for her arrest.

"For what?" I asked.

"There was a court date recently. Remember I told you I was sick?" she asked.

"Yeah, but I thought you said you told Klein's case coordinator, what's her name, Evans."

"Exactly and, I did. I know for a fact I did. Klein says I'm in contempt and she's charging me with 'failure to appear'." She was nearly whispering the information.

"What's going on? Why are you being so quiet?

"Can you not hear me?" she asked.

"Just barely, where are you?"

"You sure you wanna know?"

"Yeah, come on."

"I'm at the court house. I'm looking at the file."

"June, you're at the court house and there's a warrant out for your arrest?"

"The envelope was opened." Her whisper had emphasis "Listen to me. There's nothing in it."

"That would mean you've seen my signature. I signed right across…."

"It's your signature. It's your signature, Danny." She spoke at a normal volume for just a moment. "Write this down," she said.

"Wait a second. Where's all my notes, the records?" I couldn't talk straight. "You're telling me that you're looking at my signature? Is it ripped completely open?"

"It was ripped open at the other end of the envelope." She was sounding more frantic. "Just, can you please write this down because they're gonna want this back from me in like two seconds."

I turned over a receipt from my fastfood meal. "Go ahead."

"It says, 'Records were found in a utility closet with this case number and matching names for defendant and plaintiff. The records appear to be confidential in nature including different psychological testing and other various notes. The documents will be kept locked on the twelfth floor."

June held the receiver away. "I'm finishing up right now, I promise!"

"Who's that?" I asked.

"It's these people behind the desk that sign out the file," she said. "They keep looking at me and getting on the phone." There was a silence before resuming "Screw them. Did you write that down?"

"I got it" A drip fell from the bottom of my drink making a small splatter on the receipt "We need a copy of that because I have a letter sent to Judy Crandall from Klein saying she has locked in her own personal filing cabinet." Thinking a bit more out loud "I guess that's why they don't want to give me my records back, because it's incomplete."

"I literally don't have money that I can use for copies. Besides, they're really beginning to creep me out. I've gotta get out of here, I think."

"I'll come down there and get a copy of it. What're you doing about the warrant? Aren't you dealing with that before you leave?" I asked.

She sighed heavy. "I told Sherry I'd be at this performance. She's so excited for me to see her on stage."

"If the timing's anything like it's been in the past year, they'll be waiting for you, June."

"I'm not gonna miss it," she paused "They know I'm here right now and they know my address. What're they gonna to do, handcuff me at a children's performance?"

In fact, that's how Sherry's terror came to life. Thirty days later, June explained how the arrest took place. She stood in line with other parents, waiting until doors opened for seating. June's eye caught Sherry up high in a large window, standing with friends before the performance. June waved back and forth until Sherry saw her. June recalls the happiness of observing Sherry's free spirit among her peers. She also remembers Sherry pausing to press both of her hands together in prayer. Her hands swayed and she raised her chin to the sky before looking back down at June. "She was like a little angel, up high in the clouds." June could sense that Sherry was aware of a pending arrest.

When the doors opened, June walked past several police officers and went straight to a seat near the stage. Her heart must have been like a jack hammer throughout the performance, they waited until the very end. During the standing ovation, June turned to see two female officers at the end of the row. They both stood in the isle facing her and then motioning to come to them where she was placed in handcuffs.

Having Sherry physically present for June's "consequence" had the aim of changing Sherry's perception of her mother. Using shock language to alter her beliefs, the hope was to ultimately break down bonds.

Tenor was coaching Mr. Schultz on what resources to use and when exactly to use them. Strategic motives were more survival based at this point because the truth would show how Judge Klein's judicial discretion was really dereliction. It's critical for Tenor to keep the past hidden. There are too many documents, recordings and providers saying the same thing. And so long as she keeps burning records and stirring up accusations, there will be no change in Sherry's situation.

I contacted Judy Crandall about the records being found in a utility closet.

"I saw Klein at the court house last week and she told me she wasn't going to agree to keep the records confidential. She said if either or both parties request to see them, they can. She even said she'd put them in the court file."

"That doesn't sound good," I commented.

"It's a stretch from her original off record comments that were centered on having the records available for the next therapist," Judy said.

"Sherry still doesn't have a therapist."

"What the hell's going on here? I'll write her a letter, if nothing else maybe she'll finally end up getting treatment."

The Honorable Laurie Klein
Hoffmann County District Court

Re: Gilland v. Schultz

Dear Judge Klein,
    I am writing on behalf of Danny Dawson, whose therapeutic records were provided to you under seal. I am requesting that I be able to pick up those records so they do not remain in the file and cannot be accessed by anyone else. I would also like to know if these records have been disclosed to anyone other than you. By copy of this letter, I am notifying the attorneys involved in the case of this request.

And the Honorable Laurie Klein, who jailed Sherry's mother, wrote a swift reply:

General Court of Justice
8th Judicial District
Hoffmann County

Ms. Judy Crandall
Re: Gilland v. Schultz; 02 CVD 23055

Dear Ms. Crandall:
    I am in receipt of your letter requesting return of the records of Dr. Danny Dawson that were produced pursuant to order in the above referenced matter. Those records have and will continue to be maintained in my separate filing cabinet that I maintain for this specific purpose. They have not and cannot be accessed by anyone else but remain available for future hearing if the need arises without an additional request for production to your client.
    With kindest regards, I am

Sincerely,

Laurie Klein
The Honorable Laurie Klein

Tenor must've been aware that I had knowledge of someone finding Sherry's confidential records in a broom closet. She let the cat out, presumably not having seen the above letter from Klein, by telling Judy Crandall that the records are with the file in the custody of the clerk's office.

Judy said she had not personally laid eyes on the file but was told specifically that documents were recently put back in the envelope and resealed. She also told Judy that Klein did open and read them. Tenor was trying to make a deal by communicating like this with Judy. How will she manage to get the records out without allowing me to review it for completion? Judy emailed me the answer:

Danny,

The problem with leaving them with the clerk is that Joe may at some point ask for and be given a chance to review and copy them. That is why I want to get them out of the courthouse. He does not trust you, so will not agree to having them go back to you, but from what I understand from Darla, he may be willing to let me keep them. My guess is that he thinks they are somehow important in whatever garbage he is involved in against you and wants to be sure these records are preserved. I have no issue with preservation, but I think they are more protected in my custody than the clerk's.

Judy

Darla maintains control over that file. The board would later inform me that Tenor and Schultz called their office routinely to check on any decisions they were making about my license and livelihood. Tenor had a particular interest in whether the board would order me to release the original record to Joe Schultz. But I think it was Judy's brief letter that ignited Tenor. She seemed to be shooting while intoxicated. There was a bunch of "rainy day" information unveiled from her private investigators.

So the pattern is: make stuff up and put it in an order and then use contempt motions as a means of coercion. In this case, it was a bad thing for Mommy and Daddy or Husband and Wife to be together. Husband, wife, and child desperately wanted to see each other and when they did, the cameras were there to capture the evidence. Tenor unleashed in the following motion:

HOFFMANN COUNTYIN THE GENERAL COURT OF JUSTICE
GILLAND DISTRICT COURT DIVISION
v.02 CVD 23055
SCHULTZ

MOTION FOR TEMPORARY AND
EMERGENCY CUSTODY; MOTION
TO CHANGE THERAPIST
(MCUS)

1. Pursuant to the Temporary Custody Order, Danny Dawson was to remain the therapist for the minor child, and it was the intent of the Court that the minor child feel free to disclose secrets to Danny Dawson.
2. The Plaintiff has exercised her visitation with the minor child in the residence that she and Skip Gilland rented. She continues to sign her name "Gilland". Skip Gilland was seen interacting with Sherry at their apartment complex this summer.
3. Skip Gilland and the Plaintiff were observed kissing and hugging in the parking lot of their apartment. Further, they have been observed wearing wedding rings on more than one occasion.
4. Defendant took out a restraining order for the benefit of the minor child against Skip Gilland. Since that time, the Plaintiff has appeared in court with Skip Gilland on three separate occasions. Two of the occasions the Plaintiff and Skip Gilland sat together and wore wedding rings.
5. The Plaintiff and Skip Gilland went together to meet with Skip Gilland's lawyer for the domestic violence action.

6. The Plaintiff regularly informed Skip Gilland of the dates and substance of the child's therapy sessions with Danny Dawson. Skip Gilland began contacting Danny Dawson regularly.

7. The Plaintiff, Danny Dawson and Skip Gilland appeared in court together seeking emergency custody of the minor child. The Plaintiff failed to file a Motion for Emergency Custody and failed to disclose to Defendant or his counsel the reasons for seeking emergency custody. The Plaintiff and Danny Dawson insinuated sexual abuse of the child. Upon information and belief, the Plaintiff may have taken the child to see a medical doctor despite the court's order directing the Plaintiff not to.

8. Danny Dawson has contacted social services and attempted to have custody of Sherry removed from the Defendant. Upon information and belief the Plaintiff was involved in these attempts to have custody changed to her. A copy of a letter from Hoffmann County Human Services to Danny Dawson is attached hereto, marked as Exhibit C, and is incorporated herein by reference.

9. Skip Gilland admits that he speaks to Danny Dawson every week or two weeks and has spoken to him as recently as two weeks ago. Danny Dawson does not provide him therapy so it is reasonable to believe that they are discussing Sherry.

10. Skip Gilland interacted with Sherry in the lobby of Danny Dawson's office during at least one of her therapy sessions. Upon information and belief, this visit was facilitated by Danny Dawson and the Plaintiff.

11. Danny Dawson was found to have over-billed the Defendant for therapy and refused to reimburse the Defendant. See attached letter from SocialWell, marked as Exhibit M, attached hereto and incorporated herein by reference.

Danny Dawson is currently under investigation by the State Social Work Certification and Licensure Board for his conduct. See attached letter marked as Exhibit P, incorporated herein by reference.

12. The domestic violence restraining order against Skip Gilland was dismissed so there is a substantial likelihood that the Plaintiff will continue to allow contact between Skip Gilland and the minor child.

13. The Plaintiff threatened the Defendant that she and Danny Dawson planned to file another report to social services in an attempt to have custody changed and that Danny Dawson was going to continue to treat the child unless another therapist started treatment.

14. Plaintiff discontinued her "family therapy" as required by the court order after only two sessions.

15. The Defendant has arranged for an unbiased therapist to treat the child and the Plaintiff and Danny Dawson are preventing the child from receiving effective therapy.

16. The Plaintiff continues to undermine the Defendant's role as a parent by telling Sherry that the Defendant is her "biological" dad but that Skip Gilland is her "father."

17. This Court should enter an *ex parte* or emergency temporary custody order suspending the Plaintiff's visitation.

18. The Plaintiff's visitation with the minor child should be supervised until she demonstrates that: she is capable of being a responsible parent; can provide a safe, stable environment, and; is receiving regular successful psychological treatment.

19. *Ex Parte* temporary and permanent custody of the child should be solely with the Defendant.

20. Danny Dawson should be removed as the therapist in this case immediately and a new therapist should be appointed to treat the minor child. The therapist should not have contact with Skip Gilland.

21. The Plaintiff's sentence for contempt of court should be activated.

22. A substantial risk of injury to the child exists if she is placed in the care of the Plaintiff.

23. The Defendant is acting in good faith and has insufficient fees to defray the expenses associated with this motion.

How could defamatory remarks be signed into orders, over and over again? Tenor not only had the weight, she also had "the floor." She had much more to say about me in open court, and I never would've known had June and I stopped communicating.

But now that I was removed as the court-appointed therapist, I discontinued visits with Sherry and June. A clinical psychologist, Carolyn Swirlet, was appointed as Sherry's new therapist. I was acquainted with Dr. Swirlet; she worked "back stage" where slimy contracts are made between a lawyer and private psychologist. I knew Swirlet in the role of parent coordinator. Sherry's parent coordinator, Rene Black, never returned my phone messages. Strange to have a coordinator that refuses to return calls from the newly court-ordered therapist, don't you think?

It's because she's never seen me "back stage." DSS in Deer County understood the political underpinning in Hoffmann's circus of control. The last good faith attempt at helping Sherry, before the case changed jurisdiction, was getting her away from the biased wrath of Dr. Gandall. Deer DSS took the time to interview Sherry. The Director understands the difference between accepting a case for investigation and substantiating a case for abuse, neglect, and maltreatment. There's no harm in ruling out what is suspect, especially when it's the law. The chance of a child getting assistance hinges on whether DSS decides to follow up on the information reported.

Can intentional disregard for common sense be ticketed?

At this point, Dr. Swirlet knew nothing about this case. Maybe I could lean on the relationship to gain some insight. I was pleasantly surprised when she accepted my invitation. And, what's better? She's bringing Dr. Gandall. Here's a chance to meet Sherry's past and future psychotherapists. Both were hand-picked backstage.

XVII. Backstage Pass

"**D**r. Dawson?" came the familiar voice of Dr. Swirlet. We had shared cases and talked over the telephone but never had a face-to-face until now.

"Yes," I stood and pivoted to shake hands.

"I'm Carolyn," she said side stepping, "and this is Dr. Gandall."

"Dr. Gandall, I'm glad to meet you," I said.

Dr. Gandall extended her right hand "Please, call me Kate. It is nice to finally put a face to the name."

"Likewise," I replied.

Both were dressed casually, wearing slacks and blouses. The size differential might parallel Laurel and Hardy, quite a distinct contrast.

After a few ice-breakers about the weather, they were ready to show me around.

"I'm really excited to hear about this parent coordinator role," I was unfolding silverware from my table napkin. "I can't get a grasp on how these court-appointed roles are serving the child's best interest."

Both were nodding but neither seemed eager to take the podium.

"But it's probably because I don't know what the actual scope of the position is."

Swirlet began, "you pointed out on the phone that you see Hoffman County as being different from other counties in the state?"

"Right," I confirmed.

Gandall shook her head back and forth while swallowing some buttered bread. She didn't waste any time when the waiter placed the basket down. "That's true, Carolyn."

I will talk over this anxious presentation that Kate brought to the table.

"Yeah, the roles are much clearer. For example, the mediator versus what you guys are doing as parent coordinators…. How do you interface with a private therapist like myself?"

Swirlet seemed almost too relaxed for the topic. But it was just a good poker face. She rolled the window down further and started talking about how she had to go on "sabbatical" for a few years recently. She went on about how the stress became too much for her. Maybe Swirlet was referring to the nature of working with hostile parents. Or perhaps the contracted services were requiring long hours. Nope. It was guilt.

Swirlet spoke candidly about receiving compensation from federal program funds regulated by the Administrative Office of the Courts. The more you inquire the more it feels like a shell game. Swirlet's fingers crawled to the center of the table. And conversation stopped as if there was a technical difficulty.

I looked at Dr. Gandall, then back to Dr. Swirlet. "What?"

Swirlet was actually looking at Gandall while asking me, "Can you assure us that you'll keep this conversation confidential?"

"Geez," I said "Don't tell me anything you don't have to," I don't know why I said that because I really wanted to know everything.

"You understand that I'm getting paid by the court," she sat forward and leaned across the table.

"It was a presumption," I answered.

"And when you called, you were wondering if a parent is responsible for payment?"

I didn't think she was taking notes during our call.

"Yeah?" I felt like I was standing on thin ice.

"The parent pays for the service," was half of the story.

I started on my salad. "And the court funds pay for...what?"

"It's like a retainer for testimony, letters, parent meetings...."

"But not meetings with the child, right?" I asked.

Dr. Gandall interjected, "That's why I'm so reluctant to discuss Sherry's case."

I tilted my head in the direction of Swirlet, continuing with my salad. "I mentioned to Carolyn that we don't need to talk about the case at all today."

I figured out it was Gandall that wanted to share, after all.

"It's not so much the biological father that's a threat, it's my 'employer', if you will."

If I was getting this correctly, both of them were trying to tell me they were unethical.

With a puzzled look, I asked, "So, are you getting paid twice, then?"

Dr. Swirlet couldn't look me in the eyes just before saying, "It's what it is, Danny. I'm personally ashamed, but it's my job." Her eye contact returned, "There's plenty of times where the attorney asks me to re-review DSS records simply because they're dragging it out until one of the parents is out of money. Watch how fast services vanish when the money runs out."

"One of the parents runs out of money?" I knew the pattern.

"Oh, yeah. It's pretty easy for two attorneys to determine how a case will end up shortly after the first round of bills goes out. You've probably seen how one or even both parents have to take out loans or borrow from extended family?"

"I've seen it before, yeah," I said.

"Sure, you have," She smiled and looked more comfortable.

At this point, I thought about asking, "So you took time off to think about your contribution to a corrupt system and decided to come back for more?"

"Okay, I'm following. So far, you're giving some pieces that help put the puzzle together."

"Yeah, well, I didn't figure on it being a colleague that was going to confront us," she announced.

I'll never forget that comment. The sooner I could exhaust their knowledge bank, the sooner I could get away from these criminals. Maybe Gandall would say something if I nudged her in the right direction.

I kept thinking about my drive home and how I didn't want to regret not asking the tough questions. "What's the rate of reimbursement from the AOC compared to the private practice fee you're getting, if you don't mind me asking."

Something about that question gave our meeting some unexpected life. I think both of them thought it was a signal that I may want in on the money.

"It's $175 an hour, not including any travel expenses. Collateral contacts are billed by the quarter hour," Gandall said.

"175 billed to the parent and then 175 billed to whom, the AOC for each service?"

Gandall affirmed with a slow nod Swirlet was sporting a guilt-pressed crescent.

"Wow. That's a lot of cash," I said.

"Guess what?" Swirlet asked.

"What?"

"Judge Klein's open to having the first contracted clinical social worker, if you're interested."

"You're kidding me?" I played.

"I am not kidding you, Danny. And just take a guess at what you can make on an annual basis. Just guess." Swirlet was suddenly getting into this.

I continued to play, "I could probably get pretty close if I knew how many cases I'd be promised."

"Can you imagine six figures?" she paused. "You can't be making anything like that as a social worker. Am I right?"

"Nope. I'm not making six figures," I said.

"Trust me," Gandall was beginning to look like a shoulder angel, "I've had more than a few close calls with my practice."

"I couldn't deal with that," I risked. "I'm losing enough sleep with this that I'm going through right now."

"Here's the thing," Swirlet encouraged, "in the case of a grievance filed by anyone subsequent to work affiliated with the Family Court, a quick phone call to the case coordinator and you're fine."

I was getting an overwhelming feel from Gandall that she wasn't sharing the same level of confidence.

"We both can attest to that," Swirlet continued "The Psychology Board didn't ask us to do anything. Two letters show up: one that acknowledges receipt of the complaint and another communicating that the complaint was unfounded." She flipped her hair to the side laughing out loud, "I literally didn't have to do a thing."

Gandall was smiling, but it looked more like she had an accident. She leaned over the table and in stealth fashion says, "I've had," holding up three fingers she mouths, "three."

Swirlet didn't like Gandall making discouraging comments. I don't think they had rehearsed this meeting very well.

"But again, he needs to understand that each of those were handled seamlessly by her," she dabbed the corner of her mouth, "don't scare the child away".

I wasn't being clear enough, "Wait a minute. Both of you have had complaints filed against you? Plural?"

"Sure," Swirlet replied.

"Who's fixing these for you, a judge?"

"No," Gandall explained. "The judge gets the message from the case coordinator. We have to keep any ex parte communication to a minimum."

"Do tell more, I'm interested" It wasn't a lie; it just wasn't the whole truth.

There was an exhale in their posture.

Swirlet said, "The attorney refers the client directly to you. That's kind of like your guiding light. The attorney will know what the plan is and you just testify accordingly," she smacked.

I was trying to fit pieces together when I impulsively shared my thought out loud, "That would explain the GAL thing."

It was just a mumble. Did they hear that? Gandall and Swirlet gave me their undivided attention.

"The GAL program uses volunteers. That's not going anywhere. I've come to terms with the security of my position," Swirlet growled. She was probably wondering if they gave too much information. She was right; I didn't want to play anymore. I was ready to clean up our mess and go home.

"How did the two of you decide to do this? Let a kid go without a voice? Let a child remain in an abusive environment?" I slapped.

Gandall wasn't about to sit idle "I'll tell you it became easier for me to make a decision after being given an ultimatum," Gandall looked briefly over at Swirlet "I essentially had to agree to the expected testimony or things would go down," tapping the rim of her water glass.

"Oh, yeah," I asked "such as...?"

"Such as this case we're talking about right now where I had to accept responsibility for insurance billing. I've never had to file and didn't plan on it until Darla called me and started changing things up." She was sounding pathetic.

Here was some of the confirmation I was looking for about Schultz and Tenor. Both of them were very familiar with how his mental health benefit worked. I was likely set up from day one. Tennor had Schultz protect himself in the event of a catastrophic turn of events. If they couldn't count on the therapist's testimony, they had a bailout plan.

"Schultz used his Social Well insurance with you?" I asked Gandall.

She leaned down to open her soft briefcase but her neck was contorted as she maintained eye contact with Swirlet.

"I don't care, Linda," she barked. "I'm sick of this bullshit."

Gandall pulled out billing documents and a letter requesting reimbursement of out of pocket fees spent on Sherry's therapy. Gandall was upset for the wrong reasons.

"This was money that Darla could get back for him so that he could keep paying her after June stopped paying half the bill," she navigated. "And, if you haven't signed a contract with SocialWell, don't. Darla got plenty of miles from them but in the process, kicked me to the curb," shaking her head. "Still can't believe she did that to me."

"Oh, geez," is all that I could say.

Swirlet wasn't talking. She looked like one of those airline commercials where it says, 'need to get away?'

"Consider yourself lucky," Gandall said.

"This doesn't have anything to do with luck," I said without hesitation. I didn't have any problem watching tears run down her face.

"What about the SocialWell contract?"

Swirlet stood up from the table. "I need to excuse myself for just a moment, I'm sorry."

Gandall's eyes tracked Swirlet as she walked from our table.

"It was a tremendous amount of grief for me. I had to sort through a ton of figures and then give back money that I didn't set aside," she hesitated "I guess that wasn't mine to begin with."

Good for her, she was making progress on her 'insight' goal.

"I'm lost," was the best comment I could come up with to keep her fired up.

"Not only did I have to submit all the medical claim forms, but Social Well told me to reimburse him for my court testimony time, too," Gandall said.

"Don't you have a separate contract that Schultz signed for that?"

"When Darla has Klein backing her, she can accomplish whatever she damn well wants. One minute you're her best friend, the next minute she runs over you like road kill".

I didn't know what to think of that comment but didn't stop for a second look.

"I thought you guys were saying that Klein had your back all the time," hoping to keep the story straight.

"I left out the chain of seniority" Gandall acting as though she is writing on the table. "It goes: Judge, Attorney, THEN Parent Coordinator," she said.

"So you're disposable at any given time," I commented.

"That's for damn sure," Gandall was more frustrated than sad now "This whole ordeal was an absolute nightmare. She was so pissed with Deer DSS when they asked for Sherry to get a new therapist. I swear Darla took it out on me."

"By doing all this stuff to you?"

"By sicking SocialWell on me. I don't know if Darla offers people cash or what. I don't how she does it but, she does it. I ended up having to send Schultz a check for some large damn sum of money," she said.

I'm sure my face was showing little sign of sympathy.

Darla has channeled her frustration into Sherry's case by squeezing visitation time and becoming more invasive in June's life. The powerlessness of living within a closed system, I'm telling you, must be like a Stephen King snow globe where disbelief is common nature. Tenor, Schultz, and Klein, 'they' could watch from above as June struggled to keep a job because 'someone' would call her employer trying to discourage them from keeping her on the job. 'Someone' even interfered with her other two sons by calling DSS, accusing them of drug use and possession of paraphernalia. Tenor understood there would be no basis to substantiate such allegations, but it was instrumental in a process of disruption where the intended goal is to wear someone down until they say 'uncle'. Tenor was using whatever legal demand happened to fit in getting her what she wanted.

Gandall began gathering papers as soon as Swirlet returned.

I pointed at a single document, "Can I look at Darla's invoice to Schultz, real quick?"

Greedy, I took two. The first one was from her cell phone carrier; Tenor was seeking evidence of June's contact with Skip:

The Subpoena Processing Unit:
   Please be advised that we have received a legal demand (subpoena, Search Warrant, Summons or Court Order) for your account information. If you wish to protect your privacy, you must respond no later than December 12 with a formal objection or motion to quash filed by your attorney.

This, of course, meant that June would need more money, simply to protect her privacy rights. The other document was a line item invoice that included the following charges:

Contact with DSS intake social worker, Social Well Inc., request for records from June's cell phone carrier, a court reporting agency, Clerk 3B re court file; conversation with Judge Klein regarding obtaining DSS files; conversations with Sherry's school and; pediatrician. Watched video and reviewed PI report.

When I looked up, Swirlet had direct eye contact with me.

"You certainly have given me something to think about," she sneered.

I flagged the waiter, pointed at the table and mouthed 'check please'.

"I hope you mean that in a good way," pleasant posture sustained our interaction. She was now fully aware of my reason for meeting with her today. And she did, in fact, provide the education I needed. The bitterness was bleeding from her eyes.

There we stood outside of the restaurant. I could sense she would have message before parting ways. Sure enough, Sherry's newly appointed therapist announced her position on continuity of care: "Mr. Dawson, I will say this to you," she gave a casual smile to people going in for lunch and then put her sunglasses on to give it the full motion picture effect, "I hope I never have to speak with you again."

XVIII. If You Love Me You Will Kill Me

Sherry already had several sessions with Dr. Swirlet by the time June was released. After thirty days, June desperately wanted to see Sherry to explain what had happened. June used extended visitation time to visit her parents out of town with Sherry. And it was during this time that she called in crisis:

"She just tried to hang herself." The phone dropped to the floor, June sounded as if she was getting sick. "Sorry, I'm sorry."

"Deep and slow, June. Just two for me; breath with me for just a second, June."

"She thinks they'll put me back in jail," she gasped "She's going to use her jump rope. She had it tied outside, up on the side like, she was really gonna do it, Danny. She doesn't want to go back, but there's nothing I can do." Again, the phone dropped but right away she picked it back up.

"You need to get her seen by somebody, June."

"I talked to Swirlet and, you're not going to believe this." Her rate of speech was climbing "She never told Sherry where they took me."

"Why not?"

"Swirlet said Schultz told her Klein didn't want anyone telling her, so she made stuff up, I guess. I mean, Swirlet's telling me that Sherry was in a panic state. She watched her suffer, telling her my phone was maybe broken. *This* is who my child's new therapist is?!" Now, she was mad. "Watching her play therapy with these inflatable swords and she's acting aggressive, going around her office stabbing furniture. That's not right."

"Look, you'll need to get her to someone and have her assessed."

"She's saying really bizarre things, Danny! I need to know what to do! What do I do?!"

"June?"

She stopped, "Yeah" a short moment "I'm here. Tell me again. What do I do?"

"Look in the phone book or ask you parents if they know where the nearest ER or mental health clinic is located," I explained. "Do you want me to talk to one of them?"

"No. I'm fine, I got it," she refreshed.

"Okay. Good."

June's electric mood came back "Wait a second! Then they'll hang *me*! The order says I can't bring her to the doctor, you know that".

"Contact Swirlet, right now. I'll be blown away if she says don't get her help," I said.

"If I bring her to someone," June had a very anxious chuckle before adding "They'll say I set this whole thing up. They're not gonna believe me. They'll turn it all around and say it happened because I'm unfit," she cried.

I kept at her, "June, listen to my words. Trust me. Go to auto-pilot mode for me." I coached a bit more directly saying "Contact Swirlet immediately on whatever number she gives out for emergencies. You told me you had her pager, didn't you?"

I could only hear marathon breathing.

"June?"

"I'll do it," she committed. "I'll do it right now before I change my mind."

"Awesome, June."

I was standing in my garage on that late Saturday morning. And after hanging up the phone, I took notice of how pleasant the weather felt. The air was fresh and the temp was near perfect. I watched a set of parents and their daughter pass by the front of my house. The father was busy trying to compensate steering as the daughter wrestled to master her training wheels. I was drifted away in thought. Some things are so readily accessible yet often overlooked.

During these weeks and months, I was also dealing with the stress of my board. My attorney, Gretchen Platt, was sending documents and inquiring about when the matter might conclude. We were now well past the twelve-month marker and I had fully explained my position relative to the complaints that were filed. The board wasn't talking except to say, "There isn't a time limit." Still standing in my garage, I began feeling angry on that beautiful day. That family was nearly out of sight when I threw a tennis ball at the wall as hard as I could.

As it will go, my son happened to be watching me.

"You alright, Dad?" he asked.

I looked into his eyes and my agitation ran away.

"Will you come over here?"

His hockey stick dropped to the garage floor and we held each other for a few seconds.

"Thanks, my man," I said.

With no further questions, he picked it back up and resumed stick handling practice.

My cell rang. Noticing it was June, I picked right up.

"What'd you hear? Anything?" I asked.

"Swirlet told me to get her evaluated."

"Right on!!" I yelled.

The following letter was written by the evaluating clinician for Dr. Swirlet:

> *This letter is to serve as confirmation that Sherry Gilland was evaluated for crisis stabilization after a suicide gesture. Sherry was brought into the office by her mother, June Gilland, stating that Sherry needed someone in which she could confide her feelings regarding the changes that had occurred over the past several years.*
>
> *Sherry initially presented as quiet, calm and somewhat shy child. During the first visit, however, she became very vocal about her wishes to live with her mother instead of "Schultz," her biological father. At this point, Sherry questioned her paternity and insisted that Skip Gilland was her "real dad".*
>
> *Ms. Gilland was visibly upset and expressed concerns over Sherry's most recent behavior. It was reported by Ms. Gilland and confirmed by Sherry that she had stated that she wished that she had "never been born" and the arguing was "all her fault." Sherry admitted to stating that she was going to "hang herself with a rope so she would go to heaven with God." In*

addition, Sherry stated, "Mommy, you would kill me if you loved me. If you love me, you will kill me." Sherry admits making these comments while seated watching television with her mother.

As these feelings were processed throughout the session, Sherry finally committed to avoid any self-harming behaviors. She stated that she didn't really want to die but was often sad about her current living situation. She was verbal in her dislike regarding her current living situation with her biological father and was adamant that she would be much happier residing with her mother.

Ms. Gilland feels comfortable supervising Sherry until returning home where she is currently being treated by a clinical psychologist.

Sincerely,

Heather L. Taylor, LPC-MHSP
Clinical Director

Swirlet has not contacted me for records, and she will not return my phone messages. To date, Sherry has not been evaluated by a psychiatrist.

XIX. Narcissistic Quality

I t was a grueling two and a half years of captivity. I found myself in a similar predicament as the parents I was serving in that my pockets were empty yet the invoices kept coming. Every conversation, email response, phone call, letter or whatever else, it was all there in a similar line item format. In order to keep my practice open, I had to meet any and all demands presented by the board. And, there were many. Just as an example, the board ordered Sherry's records, but they wanted five separate copies made. That's a lot of paper and a lot of risk. I don't get to know what the board is thinking or how they arrived at certain decisions. They certainly didn't look at my CV or contact previous employers. Had they done so, they would have learned about repeat nominations, awards and other significant measurements of personal conduct such as membership satisfaction statistics. Instead, the months dragged on and communication was sparse.

One of the orders came with a fat $500.00 price tag. The unspoken message was even bigger: If the Board's Investigator was unable to substantiate Schultz's complaints, they would now begin looking for one of their own:

Social Work Board

BY CERTIFIED MAIL, RETURN RECEIPT
7006 3450 0001 8832 2579
Re: ORDER for Psychiatric Evaluation

Dear Mr. Dawson:
Within five business days of your receipt of this Order, you are ordered to contact Kurt Jennings, MD to schedule for yourself a psychiatric evaluation to address your ability to practice social work with reasonable skill and safety. Upon Dr. Jennings, you are ordered to participate in a psychological evaluation by a psychologist designated by Dr. Jennings, and/or engage in psychological testing. This evaluation is to

include: 1) substance abuse screening, 2) any evidence of global or situation-specific impaired judgment, 3) any history of personal experience that may cause or contribute to any bias in your professional abilities for or against any client populations, such as possible bias towards minor children, or against parents in conflictual relationships.

Further, you are ordered to either provide to the Board, or sign releases authorizing the Board to obtain medical, mental health, and psychiatric records from any providers who may have treated you within the last three years for any symptoms or conditions which may affect your ability to practice clinical social work. This includes current substance/drug use testing.

You are responsible for all costs associated with this evaluation. Failure to comply with this order may result in Emergency Certificate Suspension: Nothing within Paragraph (a) of this Rule shall abridge the right of the Board to take emergency actions to summarily suspend a certificate. In the event that the Board issues a Summary Suspension, your right to practice is immediately terminated, and a hearing will be held within thirty days.

I'm guessing they were disappointed when Jennings sent the following evaluation results:

PSYCHIATRIC AND SUBSTANCE ABUSE EVALUATION

Sources of Information:
Clinical interview with Mr. Dawson. I also interviewed his wife at the end of the interview.

Telephone interviews

Case materials provided by the Board. These include the formal complaint against Mr. Dawson, the Board's investigator's report, copies of two court orders, and the order for evaluation sent to Mr. Dawson.

Relevant History:

The allegations against Mr. Dawson involve not following court orders relating to Mr. Schultz's daughter, an allegation of billing fraud, and exceeding his scope of practice by acting as an advocate for Mr. Schultz's daughter, in that he called an emergency meeting with Judge Klein regarding acute symptom exacerbations. He does admit that he continued to see Sherry after being notified by Mr. Schultz that he was to cease treatment. His reason for this is that as far as he knew, there was no therapist seeing Sherry. He felt that it would potentially be abandonment and a breach of his duty to Sherry. He also cites General Statutes whereby minors are permitted to seek treatment for emotional distress and he felt that his four additional visits with Sherry fell under that statute. Regarding the issue of sexual abuse of Sherry, he admits that he was never certain that it occurred. However, he felt that it was his duty to advocate for Sherry before the court, therefore he asked for the emergency meeting with Judge Klein. He felt it would be an ethical violation if he had the question in his mind that she had been abused and not take action. Regarding the issue of not releasing the clinical record to Mr. Schultz, he says that he was entitled at any time to get a copy of his clinical record but not the psychotherapy notes. He feels that this is covered under the HIPPA law. He did in fact provide the entire record under court seal. He furthermore was unable to get previous records from Sherry's treatment. He believes that Mr. Schultz failed to get a therapist for Sherry for a period of seven months after he ceased treatment with Sherry.

An important issue for Mr. Dawson is what he sees as serious problems in the State relating to how pediatric mental health treatment is carried out. He sees serious problems relating to "interagency communications" between the Department of Health and Human Services, Child Protective Services, and Family Court. He has tried to carry his concerns not only to Judge Klein but also to the State Secretary of Social

Services, the FBI, State Senators, and other bodies. He believes State statutes are being violated and children are not getting the healthcare they are entitled to. He has presented these concerns in a peer supervision group as well. He feels that there are numerous cases where there was essentially an injustice related to the care of the child. He closed his pediatric mental health clinic over similar concerns. Despite all of his efforts, he feels helpless in the face of the lethargy that he perceives inherent in the system.

In my opinion, I do not feel that Mr. Dawson has abnormally misinterpreted or over-interpreted the concerns he has about "the system." I do believe that Mr. Dawson has seen social work as a calling. He is an individual who believes passionately in his profession. For it to be questioned has been a psychological blow. I would not recommend any further mandates in any way by the Board. I find no reason for the Board to require any further monitoring or follow up evaluations. A question has been raised about the reason or reasons why Mr. Dawson seemed to be at such odds with Judge Klein and why there developed an adversarial relationship with Mr. Schultz. It is also worth questioning why he chose to continue to see Sherry despite having been discharged by Mr. Schultz. There is a question as to whether Mr. Dawson had a narcissistic quality which caused him to carry on in this manner. I do not believe any of this to be the case. I feel that he believes strongly in the welfare of children and did have a differing opinion with that of the court. He perhaps could have handled it more diplomatically, but I believe that all of his actions were driven by his strong belief that he was acting in the best interest of Sherry. It seems to me that he has some reasonable arguments to make as to why he carried out the actions that he did and I do not find them to be colored by narcissism or other pathological personality characteristics. Mr. Dawson appears to have much to offer in the treatment of children and families, and I hope that he continues to make a positive contribution to the field of social work in our state.

I hope this information is helpful to the Board. I remain available for questions on the part of the Board.

Kurt Jennings MD

Kurt Jennings, M.D.
Board Certified in General & Addiction Psychiatry

I tend to believe that Dr. Jennings found this to be peculiar. When he was reviewing my CV he asked, "Do they have all this information about you?" My eyebrows were raised, his were lowered. Nevertheless, this put a crack in the snow globe. And several months later, a blessing arrived to wedge it open.

I was the recipient of the Legal Defense Fund Award from the National Association of Social Workers in Washington D.C.

NASW LEGAL DEFENSE FUND AWARD
Celebrating 35 Years
OF LEGAL EDUCATION
AND SUPPORT FOR
SOCIAL WORKERS

RE: NASW LDF Application

Dear Mr. Dawson:
This is to inform you that the NASW Legal Defense Fund Board of Trustees met and reviewed your application for financial assistance. The Board carefully considered your application materials and discussed the issues relating to treatment of children whose parents are involved in custody matters, consent to treatment for minors, confidentiality, and protection of children as they relate to the NASW Code of Ethics and to the practice of the social work profession.
Based most particularly on the Board members' concerns for social workers' protection of client records, the Board

voted to provide some support to your case. The LDF Board approved your application in the amount of $3,000. The approved funds will be forwarded directly to your legal counsel, Gretchen Plat, at Anderson & Burns, LLP, based on billing presented for that amount. If necessary, we will be available to discuss this with your attorney.

As per your authorization, NASW may publish information about this LDF award in future NASW NEWS or other publication with or without your identifying information. We would appreciate receiving additional information about the outcome of your case following the scheduled licensure board hearing.

Sincerely,

Associate & General Counsel
LDF and Office of Ethics and Professional Review

cc: Connie Ball, Executive Director, NASW-(State Local Chapter)

XX. Gross Advocacy

My State Licensure Board "drilled" for two years, and found nothing. I did start to feel a sense of confidence kicking in after getting the LDF (Legal Defense Fund) Award from NASW (National Association of Social Workers)—and Dr. Jennings's evaluation, which was especially supportive. Another feeling was that I could begin networking this information and build support through a consensus gathering. Eeeeeyeaaah, no. Not going to happen. I am learning, slowly. And with each whack across my knuckles, I will try to be less forgetful. The Board has absolute control over every "independent" part of every "variable." Take for example the licensee's relative feeling of confidence. It really didn't matter if my answers were right or if someone somewhere else thought I knew what I was talking about. Support has its limitations if the source is anywhere outside state lines. My Board never flinched. And maybe, to some extent, literally because when I finally met with them, it seemed as if they hadn't read any of the materials.

Mitch Richards, the Ethics Director, looked too relaxed when he opened with "Mr. Dawson, go ahead and tell us what happened."

Either they were experts at Columbo Therapy, or at the very least, a majority of committee had not read the file. Foy Dillard, the stealth fighter I spoke about earlier, he's front and center in this informal Hearing at their offices, two hours away. (I dreaded to think about next month's invoice from Gretchen.)

"Mr. Dawson, if you suspected child abuse, why didn't you report it to DSS?" Foy asked.

I kept my mouth distracted by taking a slow reach to my water glass. Gretchen wasn't talking. Maybe she's helping me out in a different kind of way. Maybe she'll keep the bill cost down by not saying much. I looked first at Foy then tried prompting Mitch because he's the guy that everything was addressed to, including those five separate copies of Sherry's confidential record.

"Mr. Dillard, I filed a report. I then appealed the unsubstantiated report with the director of child welfare. I'm sorry if that was not made available for your review."

Dillard also impressed with a sort of "post feast" posture. Until now, perhaps he felt threatened and wondered if I saw through any hair transplants. But the giant was abruptly up and at the front of his seat. He swiveled to his personal copy of the documentation. He held one of my dictionary size packets up to his neck, hesitated, and then dropped it flat on the table surface in front of him.

Maybe he *did* get my email! Remember the "reply all" thing pertaining to his firm serving as the Board's legal counsel?

"Do you think I read every page of this thing?"

Inner dialogue told me to take another drink of water.

Mitch leaned over and apparently made a validating comment to Foy because he was able to take the wheel back, even if only momentarily. "Why didn't you sign the consent order, Mr. Dawson?" Mitch confronted. "We think it's more than reasonable."

I could either end this now by signing the consent order, agreeing to a reprimand, or spend another ten thousand dollars I didn't have for representation at a formal hearing. "Because, Mr. Richards, I don't understand why I have to accept a reprimand. Is there a rule or code that was violated?" I then took out a document, passed it to Gretchen and then motioned for her to send it around the horn. Foy and Mitch looked at each other before giving a parade smile to the committee.

I explained, "Recently, I discovered that NASW requires members to alert their local chapter if they're in the process of a disciplinary action. So, I initiated a professional peer review." I paused to share a moment with reticent faces around the room; they could see there was more to the picture. "This letter that I'm passing around is a response from the National Chapter indicating that without a violation, there's no need to file for a peer review."

"National Organizations are not affiliated with State Board operations, Mr. Dawson." Mitch wasn't eager to learn about my tales from faraway places.

"Any improved continuity could only be helpful to licensees, correct?" I asked.

"Well, I believe we're closely aligned with NASW's standards," Mitch said.

"On this particular case, I don't believe so." I pulled out an additional two pages.

Gretchen's eyes widened. She wasn't in favor of bringing the LDF into it.

"Didn't you receive this, Mitch?" He remained indifferent. "It's a copy of my Legal Defense Fund Award. The language of this cover letter says something different than what you're—"

Foy's face was cherry red. He reached for a book and began to flip through pages. "You want a violation code?" he asked, his words terse.

My water glass was empty, so I bit my tongue and reached for the pitcher to stay occupied.

"Here's one…" Foy was pressing his index finger on a page while looking directly at me, "…and it states that both parent's consent is required to conduct treatment."

"I'm sorry, I don't understand," I said.

"What's not clear? You asked for a violation code and I gave you one," he sliced.

"That wasn't mentioned at any point." I was somewhat panicked and, for a moment, felt dependent on Gretchen.

He lowered his chin to peer over the top of his bifocals. "Maybe keep that in mind as we're trying to conclude this ordeal today."

"Mr. Dawson," said a voice from my left, "my name is Kara Thomas. I'm a clinician like yourself, and I, too, have had similar cases. My question is: what did you do after receiving the result of your appeal from the report that you filed with DSS?"

Well right on point, Kara. "I networked. I sought guidance among colleagues and local agencies," I answered.

"What kind of advice did you get from other LCSWs?" she asked.

"I was told to stop taking cases that involved custody matters."

Several subcommittee members quietly chuckled before Kara followed up. "And what did you choose to do with this particular case?" she paused. "You continued to see her didn't you?"

"I continued to provide services until an order was entered that dismissed my role as her therapist."

Kara put her glasses on and began looking over some notes. I had my doubts that Ms. Thomas would find what she wanted in the few papers in front of her. She needed the big-boy dictionary version, like Foy's and Mitch's.

Kara looked over at Mitch, "Was Mr. Dawson court appointed?"

Mitch was leaning back in his chair, and the only thing missing was a jumbo-sized bucket of popcorn. "I believe so. Yes, he was..." Mitch mumbled.

Not that I had credibility, but I was nodding my answers on Mitch's behalf as she continued to seek clarification on a variety of issues.

Kara moved on, saying, "It says in your statement where you rejected the Board's consent order, and I quote 'Mr. Dawson is eager to understand how the Board prefers he handle similar cases in the future'?"

"Yes," I acknowledged.

"Would you be interested to hear how I'd handle this, then?" Kara asked.

"I would, Ms. Thomas. Thank you."

"Simply put, the scope of practice ends when you receive the DSS letter," she said. "What about our standards?"

"That's exactly my point." She let her glasses hang. "You're calling this advocacy, correct?" she asked.

"Yes."

"There's a point at which you can begin to do harm. That's the standard, Mr. Dawson. In other words, you can never advocate."

She was harmless.

"I believe I understand," and does not mean anything more than just that, "but also the specific NASW Standards in Child Welfare. I know you're familiar with all of them, but I'm zeroing in on 4 and 5." I gave a huge smile to Mitch when I saw him look up "What's interesting is we're actually talking about Standard 4 right now—Advocacy." Luckily, Foy also made eye contact at that moment so I was able to share the same billboard smile with him.

I looked at Kara's nameplate for good luck and said, "With all due respect, Ms. Thomas, the law sets the boundary on advocacy. With kids, it's always worked best to have a relationship with at least a few good men *inside* law enforcement." Oh geez. Did that come across as "narcissistic" or maybe "chauvinistic"?

"And then what?" Foy asked.

"It really bumps over to how they deal with things from their own discipline, but it gives me confidence, especially in those emergent moments where you can feel compelled to utilize every square inch of that boundary Kara is referring to."

Kara actually seemed impressed. She didn't look defensive in the least bit, almost interested. "Just curious, you also mentioned Standard 5?" she asked.

"It's titled Knowledge Requirements, and it identifies three areas of assessment: child development, family dynamics, and the local systems." I don't know if Foy wanted to challenge me, but I'm telling myself that he, too, was becoming interested in what I had to say. I could be wrong.

"And...?" Rolling his hand in the air, his voice amplified, "Can you be more specific as to how that applies to what we're talking about on this case?"

"The Standard's language is written perfectly, do you mind if I just read directly from it?" I asked.

"Can you say it in less than two minutes?" Foy asked.

"I can do that," I replied.

"Knock yourself out" he smirked.

Bullhorn in hand, the gate had opened, and the floor was mine. I didn't take my eyes off the paper in front of me. Then I said, "Child development includes the effects of deprivation of parental care and partial separation from parents, issues of bonding and attachment. Also included in child development are parenting issues, specifically rights of parents; parental feelings and attitudes associated with asking for help in relation to or the impact of family dynamics. And family dynamics includes..." I looked up momentarily to see Foy running his hands through his hair "...the evaluation of risk, assessment of emotional aspects of parent-child relationships and problems involved in divided allegiance in cases of parental conflict, and then finally, community and local systems. That includes legal and judicial structures; processes and practices; relationships among federal, state, and local agencies; interrelationship between individual, family, neighborhood, and community; the appropriate use of media to promote public awareness of the needs of children where the client resides."

Foy stiff-armed the microphone from me. "And with that, I apologize, but we must draw this to a close. We are over our time limit." Looking at his wristwatch, he added, "Quite frankly, we'll probably need to offer one of the small offices for Gretchen and Mr. Dawson if additional time is needed."

Foy's superficial shuffling left me in a pressured quandary. Any further communication was kinked through a chain lock. How could this be the end of the meeting? I stood with my hand on my forehead and said, "I can't believe we're concluding this without—"

"Mr. Dawson, we can be done with this today. I think I speak on behalf of everyone in the room when I say that we're all eager to see this resolved. I'm sure you can agree, given how hard this has been for you."

Empathy?

"This has been on my mind morning, noon, and night, sir."

"We can appreciate that, Mr. Dawson. And the consent order's a way of bringing this to a conclusion. A formally structured peer consultation's all we're talking about. It's an opportunity to talk about how to approach similar cases in the future." Foy's hand guided me back to Ms. Thomas. "And it's really nothing more than what you're doing here today in this discussion with Kara."

My voice and eyes were straining. I thought about the expense to my family, to my livelihood, and to the families I served. I couldn't help myself from asking about their bullying tactics.

"Mitch, you indicated that Dr. Jennings would explain the reason for me having to go through such an expensive evaluation, and I never did find out. Is now a good time to explain why I had to spend $500.00 for something that he says I didn't need?"

"No, it's not. Like I said, we have another complaint matter waiting to get in this room."

"Did the members of this subcommittee have a copy of my evaluation?"

"Absolutely not, that information is held in strict confidence," Mitch said.

"I give you authorization to share the results of the complete evaluation, with anyone on this committee."

Gretchen leaned in and whispered, "You don't need to do this."

I shifted from foreground to background. I had a carousel of images that were just a blink away at any given moment. Some of these I held tightly to access my adrenaline, refresh and then recalibrate. Advocacy took shape in many ways, all of which were safe and legal. Just one blink, a child without a voice. "Did you know that Dr. Jennings felt like what information he did receive was limited to fairly incriminating things. You guys didn't give him any part of my complaint response, did you?"

"We're following the guidelines as they are set out, Mr. Dawson." Mitch shuffled. "I will tell you that there are multiple parts of the investigation. Some of what you're experiencing might seem confusing, only because you're not privy to all the parts."

"Will I then, at some point, have the opportunity to find out anything about these other parts? Would that be due process?"

Mitch continued to pacify me with active listening skills. Meanwhile, Foy managed to lube a few sentences with Gretchen. Shortly thereafter, I was in her Beemer heading back home.

"Personally, I think they're setting it up for you so that you can sue Schultz for any damages to your practice," Gretchen said. "They're fed up with both of them. He and Darla apparently call them almost every day hoping to hear you'll never practice again."

"What's the bottom line here, Gretchen?" I asked.

"The bottom line is we either send another revised consent order or start preparing for a formal hearing."

I was confused and plenty upset. "Before this meeting today, you were saying there's nothing to bring this to a formal hearing. You've been advising that I not sign on for anything that brands me with professional misconduct. I'm with you on that, but have you changed your mind?" I asked.

She pulled off to get gas and turned the engine off. "Danny, if they want to find something on you, they will."

"You're talkin' about this consent for treatment from both parents that Foy hurled at me?"

Gretchen confirmed with a stoic stare, "If it isn't that, it'll be something else."

I kept eye contact, hoping she'd have a 'but' statement or some kind of alternative that made sense. I had two solid hours of thinking time on the ride home, but it wasn't until the next day that a decision presented itself, naturally.

XXI. To The Very Best Man

It's a message inscribed on a gift I gave to my dad on my wedding day. He died after battling with the complications of diabetes and kidney failure. He was familiar with my predicament, and while definitely supportive, he reminded me of how "crusades" can impose serious collateral damage. I didn't know how long it would be before my focus would improve, but I felt too vulnerable being under the board's microscope while coping with the loss of my best man.

"Gretchen?"

"Hi, Danny, got an answer about the hearing for me already?" she asked.

"I'm ready to sign." I surrendered.

"Are you serious?!"

"My dad died, Gretchen. I'm having a hard time seeing straight."

"Danny, I'm sorry. Do whatever you need to do and I'll get an updated consent order put together."

"As soon as you've got it, let me know. I'd like to be done with it before going out of town, if possible," I requested.

And so, the complaint matter was finalized. The procedures haven't been clarified and the same child population remains at risk. Sherry resides with Joe and Diane Schultz. June was recently assaulted by Joe while at a session with Dr. Swirlet. Despite the CT scan supporting the damage Joe did to her face, the magistrate chose to focus on a cup of water June threw. The altercation occurred after June was contacted by the school counselor regarding Sherry's self-injurious behavior. Subsequently, an emergency custody hearing ordered supervised visitation. Each of the visits was located in a designated facility equipped with a meter maid.

Sherry was one of many, as I've said. Advocacy will continue through a "show and tell" format until appropriate changes are implemented. The "press" is on, revealing similar cases, until the system's sign finally reads: "OPEN."

www.ingramcontent.com/pod-product-compliance
Lightning Source LLC
Chambersburg PA
CBHW021953170526
45157CB00003B/964